STUDENT UNIT GUIDE

NEW EDITION

AQA A2 Economics Unit 4
The National and International Economy

Ray Powell

 PHILIP ALLAN

Philip Allan Updates, an imprint of Hodder Education, an Hachette UK company, Market Place, Deddington, Oxfordshire OX15 0SE

Orders
Bookpoint Ltd, 130 Milton Park, Abingdon, Oxfordshire OX14 4SB
tel: 01235 827827
fax: 01235 400401
e-mail: education@bookpoint.co.uk
Lines are open 9.00 a.m.–5.00 p.m., Monday to Saturday, with a 24-hour message answering service.
You can also order through the Philip Allan Updates website: www.philipallan.co.uk

ISBN 978-1-4441-4833-6

First printed 2012
Impression number 5 4 3 2
Year 2015 2014 2013 2012

Cover photo: Alex Yeung/Fotolia

Typeset by Integra, India

Printed in Dubai

Hachette UK's policy is to use papers that are natural, renewable and recyclable products and made from wood grown in sustainable forests. The logging and manufacturing processes are expected to conform to the environmental regulations of the country of origin.

Contents

● The exam's assessment objectives ● Answering data-response questions
● Answering essay questions ● The synoptic requirement of the ECON 4 examination ● The four key skills ● Evaluation and levels of skill mark schemes ● Stretch and challenge ● Achieving an A* grade
● Understanding UMS marks ● The exam questions in this Guide

Getting the most from this book

Examiner tips
Advice from the examiner on key points in the text to help you learn and recall unit content, avoid pitfalls, and polish your exam technique in order to boost your grade.

Knowledge check
Rapid-fire questions throughout the Content guidance section to check your understanding.

Knowledge check answers

1   Turn to the back of the book for the Knowledge check answers.

Summary

Summaries

● Each core topic is rounded off by a bullet-list summary for quick-check reference of what you need to know.

Questions & Answers

Exam-style questions

Examiner comments on the questions
Tips on what you need to do to gain full marks, indicated by the icon **e**.

Sample student answers
Practise the questions, then look at the student answers that follow each set of questions.

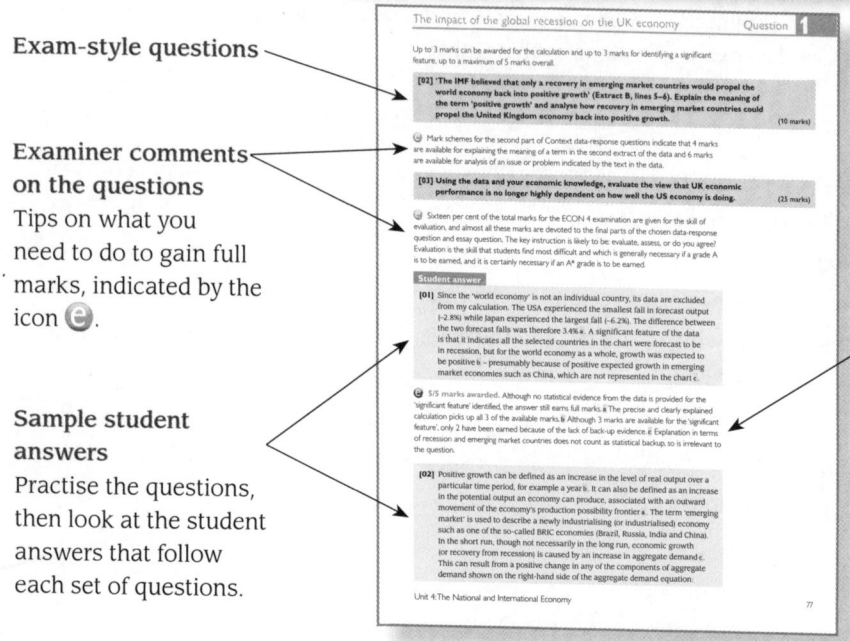

Examiner commentary on sample student answers
Find out how many marks each answer would be awarded in the exam and then read the examiner comments (preceded by the icon **e**) following each student answer. Annotations that link back to points made in the student answers show exactly how and where marks are gained or lost.

About this book

The aim of this guide is to prepare students for the AQA Advanced Subsidiary ECON 4 examination assessing **Unit 4: The National and International Economy**.

Content Guidance

Start off by reading the Content Guidance section of the book, which divides the Unit 4 specification into nine separate topics. You can read all the topics, one by one, before proceeding to the Questions and Answers section of the Guide. Alternatively, you may decide to read a particular topic and then to read the part of the Questions and Answers section that relates to the topic. The topics generally follow the order of the Unit 4 specification. Following an introductory background topic on the growth of modern macroeconomics, the topics cover the standard macroeconomic topics in the Unit 4 specification, proceeding from national topics such as economic growth and economic cycles to the international topics of trade, globalisation, the balance of payments and exchange rates. Contents Guidance also revisits and develops core macroeconomic theory originally learnt at AS: namely, the *AD/AS* macroeconomic model, and explanations of inflation and unemployment.

Questions & Answers

You should read the Questions & Answers section of the book after reading all nine specification topics in the Content Guidance section, or bit by bit, having revised a selected topic covering a particular part of the specification.

Data-response questions (DRQs)

There are four data-response questions (DRQs) in the Questions and Answers section of the Guide. In this Guide, the data-response questions are numbered 1 to 4. Questions 1 and 2 are Global Context questions, while Questions 3 and 4 are European Union Context questions. In Section A of the ECON 4 exam that you will eventually sit, the questions will be numbered **Question 1: The Global Context** and **Question 2: The European Union Context**.

The section covering the data-response questions also includes:
- A student's answer for each DRQ.
- Examiner's comments on each student's answer explaining, where relevant, how the answer could be improved. These comments are denoted by the icon **ⓔ**.

Essay questions (EQs)

Section B of the ECON 4 exam paper includes three essay questions numbered **Essay 1**, **Essay 2** and **Essay 3**, of which you must answer one question. There are also three essay questions (EQs) in the Essay questions section of this Guide. Unlike the DRQs, the essay questions, which in this Guide are numbered Questions 5, 6 and 7, do not reflect the Global and European Union Contexts which provide the format for Section A of the exam paper.

You can use each of the seven data-response and essay questions in this Guide, either as timed test questions in the lead-up to the examination, or to reinforce your understanding of the specification subject matter, topic by topic, as you proceed through the Content Guidance.

Using other Economics resources

This Guide should be used as a supplement to other resources, such as class notes, textbooks, *Economic Review* magazine and *AS/A-Level Economics Exam Revision Notes*. (The last two of these are published by Philip Allan Updates.) As this Guide contains summaries rather than in-depth coverage of all the topics in the specification, you should not use the Guide as your sole learning resource during the main part of the course. However, you may well decide to use the Guide as the key resource in your revision programme. You are strongly advised to make full use of the Questions and Answers section, especially in the revision period when you should be concentrating on improving your examination skills.

Note: AQA now provides all its resources, including the specification, past exam papers and mark schemes, on its website: **www.aqa.org.uk**.

In addition, provided they are registered with e-AQA, your teachers can also access exam papers, mark schemes and examination reports rather earlier, after the exams have finished. Any further information about AQA economics can be obtained from the Economics subject officer, AQA, Stag Hill House, Guildford, GU2 7XJ.

Content guidance

Introduction to the specification

In contrast to AS Unit 2: The National Economy, which is concerned with elementary macroeconomics, **Unit 4: The National and International Economy** centres for the most part on more advanced macroeconomics. As the specification states, Unit 4 builds on the knowledge and skills learnt in Unit 2. It requires you to use and evaluate more complex macroeconomic models than those introduced in Unit 2, and to develop further your critical approach to economic models and methods of enquiry. Nevertheless, you should be aware that, as in Unit 2, the **aggregate demand/ aggregate supply (AD/AS) macroeconomic model** is the most important of all the models you need to know and to apply in your economic analysis. The *AD/ AS* model is an essential part of the theoretical toolkit needed when analysing and evaluating the problems, puzzles or issues posed by a question.

Phillips curve analysis, both in the short run and the long run, is also required for answering Unit 4 examination questions. This is a completely new part of the specification which does not figure in Unit 2, except in the narrow sense of awareness of a conflict between macroeconomic objectives.

Unlike in Unit 2, and as the Unit title indicates, international economics is an important part of Unit 4. The main international topics you are expected to know are trade theory, the case for import controls, the balance of payments, exchange rates and globalisation.

You must appreciate the ways in which developments in the United Kingdom economy and government macroeconomic policy can be related to the Global and European Union (EU) Contexts.

Examples of issues which could be examined in the Global Context are: externally generated demand-side economic shocks, such as recession in the USA, or Japan and the Far East; externally generated supply-side economic shocks, such as the effect of global natural disasters; changes in world trade and global patterns of trade; World Trade Organization (WTO) decisions; and the global movement of capital affecting the UK balance of payments and exchange rate.

The Unit 4 specification mentions a number of examples of issues in the European Union Context which might form the scenario for an EU Context data-response question. These are: the EU as a trading bloc (customs union) and the Single European Market (SEM); the effect of the free movement of capital within the EU; the single European currency (the euro) and the euro area (eurozone); Economic and Monetary Union (EMU); macroeconomic performance in other EU countries; and free movement of labour within the EU.

Summary of the specification

The AQA specification for Unit 4 contains the following sections.

3.4.1 Macroeconomic indicators

Unit 2 introduced you to the economy's **actual growth rate** and its **trend growth rate**, and to the fluctuations around the trend rate of growth associated with the **economic cycle**. At A2 you must be able to apply at least two theoretical explanations of the economic cycle, although the specification is not prescriptive of what the explanations should be, apart from noting how **supply-side** or **demand-side shocks** can trigger cyclical fluctuations. Detailed theories of economic growth are *not* required.

It is necessary to understand the costs and benefits of economic growth, and the use and limitations of national income as an indicator of changes in living standards. You must be able to discuss the impact of growth on individuals and the environment. Knowledge of the sustainability of growth is needed, which implies an understanding of resource depletion and degradation.

You are expected to interpret different types of national income data, possibly for a range of countries, but you do not need to know technical details of national income accounts. You must be familiar with different types of data, such as GDP statistics and the United Nation's Human Development Index (HDI). You may be asked to use GDP and HDI data to compare living standards in different countries.

This section of the specification also builds on the knowledge acquired in Unit 2 on the **types** or **causes of unemployment** and **demand-side** (demand-pull) and **supply-side** (cost-push) **causes of inflation**. Both unemployment and inflation need to be analysed in the *AD/AS* theoretical framework. *AD/AS* needs to be understood in greater detail than in Unit 2, particularly with reference to the **natural rate of unemployment** and **Phillips curve analysis**. As with *AD/AS*, you must understand the difference between short-run and long-run Phillips curves. Neither **consumption** nor **investment** is mentioned in the Unit 4 specification, but along with the **national income multiplier**, they may be tested synoptically.

Along with other explanations of inflation, you must know the **quantity theory of money** as a special case of demand-pull inflation. The specification states that students should understand and evaluate the **monetarist model of inflation**, which implies some knowledge of the role of **expectations** in the inflationary process. You must also know how **index numbers** are calculated and used to **measure inflation**, and the effects of inflation on individuals and the performance of the economy.

3.4.2 Managing the national economy

The Unit 4 specification requires knowledge and understanding of **monetary policy**, **fiscal policy** and **supply-side policy** as three of the main ways of managing the national economy. You need to study all these in greater detail and with more rigour than for AS. You must also appreciate the **exchange rate** as a target and instrument of monetary policy, and the interrelationships between fiscal and monetary policy.

You should understand the relationship between interest rates and the exchange rate and how the exchange rate influences policy objectives, such as inflation, unemployment and the balance of payments. Your knowledge of the conflicts between policy objectives should be more sophisticated at A2 than at AS.

Particular knowledge of the role of the **Monetary Policy Committee** of the Bank of England is required, especially in the context of its history of hitting or failing to hit the **inflation rate target** set by the government. Detailed knowledge of financial markets is *not* necessary, but you do need to understand that **bank deposits**, which are the main component of the money supply, are liabilities of the private enterprise banking system. Since it is unable to control bank deposits directly, the Bank of England attempts to influence monetary conditions via the effect of the **interest rate** on the general public's desire to hold bank deposits. Detailed knowledge of the money supply is no longer required, but knowledge of a recent development in monetary policy known as **quantitative easing** is expected.

With regard to fiscal policy, the specification states the need for awareness of the introduction of **fiscal rules**. The specification was written before the suspension of the UK Code for Fiscal Stability in the recessionary conditions of 2008. However, knowledge of recent fiscal conditions in the global, EU and UK economies is needed. Some knowledge of the **sovereign debt problem** and the role within the UK of the **Office for Budget Responsibility** (established in 2010) should prove useful, though neither is yet mentioned in the specification. You must also appreciate how, at the macroeconomic level, supply-side fiscal policy has become the major element of wider supply-side economic policy, and appreciate recent changes in the respective importance of demand-side and supply-side fiscal policy, particularly in the context of successive governments attempting to avoid recession and stimulate economic recovery. Some knowledge of taxation is also required, including an understanding of the canons of taxation and the microeconomic effects of changes in individual taxes.

3.4.3 The international economy

The international economy is covered in much greater depth in the Unit 4 specification than in the Unit 2 specification. Unit 4 requires knowledge of the **benefits of international trade** and the principle of **comparative advantage**, together with the possible costs of **international specialisation**.

Because of the 'context' format of the data-response questions, **globalisation** and the **European Union** are obviously important in this part of the specification. Globalisation should be given special attention via its effects, for good and for bad, on trade and the location decisions of multinational or transnational corporations. **Theories of protectionism** must be put into a European context related to the European Union as a **customs union**. Knowledge of the advantages and disadvantages of **Economic and Monetary Union (EMU)** and the **single European currency** (the **euro**) are also important.

Coverage of trade theory must include **patterns of trade** between the UK and the rest of the world. Some knowledge of the **capital account of the balance of payments** is also needed, but not in technical detail. However, the nature and significance of both **short-term** and **long-term international capital flows** should be understood.

You must revise the current account of the balance of payments learnt for the AS course, and link current account deficits and surpluses, together with capital flows, to the exchange rate. Knowledge of both freely floating and fixed exchange rates is required, together with their links to interest rates and monetary policy and to domestic macroeconomic policy and conflicts.

Checklist of relevant Unit 2 terms

Here is a checklist of Unit 2 AS terms, concepts and theories, for the most part not mentioned in the Unit 4 specification, which might be needed for the ECON 4 exam:

- the meaning of national income and output, and its measurement: GDP
- understanding data in the form of index numbers and other forms of data presentation
- the distinction between nominal and real economic variables
- the objectives of a government's macroeconomic policy: full employment, growth, controlling inflation, a satisfactory balance of payments
- the economic cycle, booms, recessions, trend growth and actual growth, output gaps
- some of the main causes (types) of unemployment
- excess demand and rising costs as causes of inflation
- the role of monetary policy (interest rates) in controlling inflation
- the meaning of aggregate demand and aggregate supply
- using the *AD/AS* macroeconomic model to analyse events taking place in the economy, the level of economic activity and the effect of government intervention and policy
- components of aggregate demand and their effect on economic activity: consumption, investment, government spending and exports
- leakages or withdrawals of demand from the economy: saving, taxation and imports
- fiscal policy used both as a demand-side policy to manage aggregate demand and as a supply-side policy to improve the efficiency and competitiveness of markets and to shift the *LRAS* curve to the right
- supply-side policies to make labour and goods markets function more efficiently and competitively
- the current account of the balance of payments
- the effect of the exchange rate on the economy

The growth of modern macroeconomics

These notes, which relate to AQA specification sections 3.4.1 and 3.4.2, prepare you to answer AQA examination questions on:

- the approach of Keynesian and free-market economists to how the economy works
- the changing views of economists regarding the major objectives of macroeconomic policy

Essential information

The Keynesian revolution

These notes provide an overview of how macroeconomics has changed in recent economic history. More than any other individual, **John Maynard Keynes** created modern macroeconomics. Until monetarism in the 1970s, macroeconomics and **Keynesian economics** were much the same thing, growing out of Keynes's great and influential book, *The General Theory of Employment, Interest and Money*, published in 1936. Before Keynes, most economists belonged to the neo-classical or pre-Keynesian school (what is now often called the free-market school). Pre-Keynesian economists believed that market forces operating in competitive markets provide a self-adjusting mechanism, which, in the long run, automatically ensures full employment and economic growth.

The pre-Keynesian or free-market explanation of employment and unemployment

Figure 1 illustrates the pre-Keynesian explanation of employment and unemployment, in which full employment is determined as the level of employment where the aggregate demand for labour equals the aggregate supply of labour, at the wage W_{FE}. According to this theory, **classical** or **real-wage** **unemployment** is caused by wage rates being too high, at W_1 rather than W_{FE}.

Pre-Keynesians believed that real-wage unemployment is temporary. Market forces would cure the problem by bidding down wages until the number of workers willing to work equals the number that firms wish to hire.

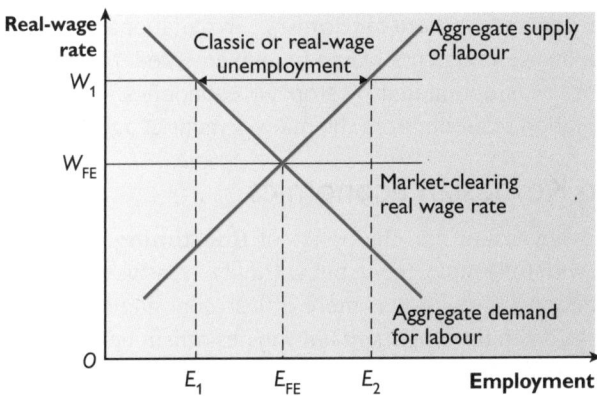

Figure 1 The pre-Keynesian theory of unemployment

Keynes's attack on the free-market explanation of employment and unemployment

In the 1930s, at the time of the Great Depression, the market mechanism failed to cure unemployment. If an individual employer, or all the firms in a particular industry, cut wages in a single labour market within the economy, more workers are hired. Aggregate demand for output is little affected if the firm or industry is only a tiny part

Real wage From workers' points of view, the real wage is the purchasing power of their money wage (nominal wage); it represents the goods that the money wage can buy. From employers' points of view, the real wage is the real cost of hiring workers. The real wage is calculated by dividing the money wage by the average price level.

Knowledge check 1

Define in single sentences the terms *employment* and *unemployment*.

Knowledge check 2

What is a free-market economy?

Great Depression The very deep recession suffered throughout the world in the 1930s.

of the whole economy. But at the macro level, if real wages are cut throughout the economy, aggregate demand falls and firms cannot sell their output. Wage cuts may therefore increase rather than reduce unemployment.

Keynes argued that **deficient aggregate demand** causes unemployment. The paradox of thrift explains this. Saving (or thrift), regarded as a virtue at the individual level, becomes a vice at the aggregate level if people save too much and spend too little.

Keynes's policy solution to unemployment

Keynes's policy solution to the problem of persistent mass unemployment was to inject demand back into the economy to eliminate deficient aggregate demand caused by saving too much and spending too little. Keynes argued that in its **fiscal policy**, the government should run a **budget deficit** (i.e. set $G > T$). In essence, the government borrows the excess savings of the private sector, which it spends itself, thereby injecting demand back into the economy and preventing the emergence of deficient demand.

The Keynesian era

The Keynesian era began shortly after 1945 when governments started to use demand management policies to achieve the objective of full employment. The era ended in the 1970s with the advent of monetarism and the free-market or new-classical revival. In the intervening 30 years, governments in many industrial countries, including the United Kingdom, used fiscal policy to manage aggregate demand. When unemployment was high, the government expanded demand by increasing the budget deficit. As full employment was approached, increased demand caused imports to rise and the current account of the balance of payments to deteriorate. It also triggered demand-pull inflation since, in the short run at least, output could not rise to meet the increase in demand. A contractionary or deflationary policy of increased taxation and public spending cuts would be implemented. Macroeconomic policy in the Keynesian era was dominated by stop–go economics — successive periods of deflation and reflation resulting from the management of aggregate demand.

The crisis in Keynesian economics

For much of the Keynesian era, the policy of **fine-tuning** aggregate demand to a level consistent with full employment, but without excessive inflation, appeared to be working, and economic growth was more or less continuous. But at the same time, inflation began to creep up. Opponents of Keynesianism became more confident in their criticism of Keynesian theories and policies, arguing that Keynesian demand management could achieve full employment only through injecting greater and greater doses of inflation into the economy. Once achieved, full employment was becoming less and less sustainable.

By the mid-1970s Keynesianism was in disarray. Keynesian theory had been relatively invulnerable to serious attack as long as Keynesian economic management performed reasonably well when measured against the main objectives of economic policy: full employment, growth, control of inflation and a satisfactory balance of payments. Keynesianism became vulnerable to attack when a simultaneous failure to achieve any of the primary policy objectives occurred in the mid-1970s. The **stagflation** (slumpflation) of stagnant or declining output and growing unemployment combined with accelerating inflation, together with social conflict over the distribution of income and a deteriorating balance of payments, signalled the end of the Keynesian era.

The monetarist or free-market counter-revolution

The 1970s witnessed the decline of Keynesianism and the ascendancy of **monetarism**. Monetarists believe that the immediate cause of all inflation lies in a prior increase, permitted by governments, of the money supply.

Monetarism began in 1956 when Professor Milton Friedman revived the old pre-Keynesian theory of inflation, the **quantity theory of money**. The quantity theory argues that the quantity of money in the economy determines the price level and the rate of inflation. If the government allows the money supply to expand at a rate faster than the growth of output, the price level rises when people spend the excess money balances they hold.

Monetarist economic policies

Monetarist policies were implemented in the UK in the late 1970s and the early 1980s. The government abandoned discretionary demand management policies and based policy on automatic policy rules. The monetary policy rule centred on the publication of a target rate of growth of the money supply for a medium-term period of about 3 years ahead, accompanied by the announcement that monetary policy would be implemented to hit the money supply target. Other aspects of macro policy, including full employment as the major policy objective, were subordinated to the monetary policy aim of controlling monetary growth in order to achieve the new prime policy objective of controlling inflation. The government also adopted a fiscal policy rule based on reducing the size of public sector spending and borrowing as proportions of national output. Fiscal policy became subordinated to the needs of monetary policy — a situation that, except in the recession of 2008 and 2009, still generally exists today.

The decline of monetarism and the growth of supply-side economics

Monetarism never really worked, with the growth in the money supply often outstripping the growth in prices. This unfortunate fact cast great doubt on the central assumption of narrow monetarism: namely, that an increase in money supply causes inflation. But although the strictly 'monetarist' aspects of macroeconomic policy were quietly dropped after the mid-1980s, later UK governments have remained committed to the wider free-market aspects of economic policy adopted during the monetarist era. In particular, **supply-side economics** came to the fore, which aimed to improve the economy's supply side and its ability to produce.

Recent developments in macroeconomic policy

Policy before the 2008 recession

For several years before the onset of recession in 2008, monetary policy was again being used (via interest rate changes) to manage aggregate demand. At this time, fiscal policy was used primarily as a supply-side policy and not for managing aggregate demand.

Examiner tip

Be aware that in recent years, economists have feared the return of stagflation, a phenomenon previously experienced during the crisis in Keynesian economics in the 1970s

Examiner tip

Don't confuse the word *monetarism* with the term *monetary policy*. Can you explain the difference? See page 40 for an explanation.

Examiner tip

ECON 4 exam questions frequently focus on supply-side economics and supply-side policies. By contrast, monetarist economic policies have seldom been referred to in ECON 4 exams. However, as the word 'monetarist' (but not monetarism) and the quantity theory of money are in the specification, you need to understand what they mean.

Policy during the recession in 2008 and 2009

However, in the panic conditions induced by recession in 2008, for a short while at least, *both* monetary policy and fiscal policy were used to manage aggregate demand. In conditions of near-zero interest rates, further cuts in the Bank of England's interest rate (Bank Rate) become ineffective as a means of stimulating aggregate demand. This was partly because, as Bank Rate was cut and fell close to zero, it became impossible to cut it below zero. In 2009 and again in 2011, monetary policy switched briefly away from interest changes into a policy of **quantitative easing** (which is akin to printing more money in the hope that people will then spend it). At the same time, fiscal policy reverted to the Keynesian use of a growing budget deficit (called a **fiscal stimulus**) to pump spending into the economy to stimulate aggregate demand.

Policy after 2009

In 2010, the outgoing Labour government's fiscal stimulus was replaced by the incoming Coalition Government's opposite policy of **fiscal austerity**. The tax cuts, public spending increases and growing budget deficit that were at the heart of the fiscal stimulus gave way to tax increases, swingeing public spending cuts and an attempt greatly to reduce the size of the budget deficit. A number of factors explain the sudden change of policy. These include the following:

- The Labour government believed it could successfully manage aggregate demand using Keynesian fiscal policy. The Coalition government (dominated by the Conservatives) rejected this and had much greater faith in how free-market forces could lead to sustained recovery from recession.
- A dramatically new problem, known as the sovereign debt **problem**, suddenly emerged, which forced *all* governments, including the UK government, to adopt policies to cut budget deficits, whether they liked to or not. Because of the sovereign debt problem, international financial markets from which governments borrow are no longer prepared to lend huge sums of money to finance budget deficits.

At the time of writing (autumn 2011), the policy of fiscal austerity may be preventing recovery from recession, leading possibly to a 'double-dip' (W-shaped) recession. At best, in the years ahead, the UK may exhibit little or no economic growth, high unemployment and possibly relatively high inflation, and the return of stagflation.

Examination questions and skills

AQA economics examinations *do not* test knowledge of events more than about 10 years before the examination. Nevertheless, it is a good idea to possess such knowledge, if only to make better sense of current and very recent policies, and of events in the UK and world economies.

Common examination errors

- Failing to understand the major objectives of macroeconomic policy, and the ways in which their relative importance has changed.
- Confusing policy objectives and policy instruments.
- Treating Keynesianism and fiscal policy as interchangeable terms.
- Treating monetarism and monetary policy as interchangeable terms.

Examiner tip
In an ECON4 exam question, the term 'fiscal restraint' may be used. It means the same as fiscal austerity.

Sovereign debt
The debt of national governments, accumulated when they borrow on international financial markets to finance government budget deficits.

- Failing to appreciate the difference between discretionary economic policy and automatic policy rules.
- A lack of awareness of recent changes in methods used to manage the macro economy.

Summary

- The Keynesian revolution occurred in the 1930s when the famous British economist John Maynard Keynes attacked the then orthodox neo-classical or free-market theory and replaced it with a new body of macroeconomic theory.

- The Keynesian era occurred at a later date, primarily in the 1950s and 1960s when economists inspired by Keynes (known as the Keynesians) implemented policies that centred on the management of aggregate demand. During this period, Keynesianism was the new orthodoxy.

- In the 1970s, the crisis in Keynesian economics occurred. Keynesian policies no longer seemed to work and Keynesianism was replaced by a pro-free-market revival.

- The free-market revival, which largely extends to the present day, became associated first with monetarism, and then with supply-side economics.

- The deep recession that occurred in 2008 and 2009 led to a short-lived Keynesian revival, centring on the return of demand-side fiscal policy and a growing budget deficit as a tool to stimulate aggregate demand.

- In the UK, a change of government in 2010 and the emergence of the sovereign debt problem put paid to the Keynesian revival. Policies involving *fiscal austerity* have replaced the *fiscal stimulus* of 2008 and 2009.

- However, the severe cuts in public spending that form the core of fiscal austerity policies may lead at worst to a double-dip recession, and at best to a period of very slow economic recovery and possibly to the return of stagflation.

Economic growth, the economic cycle and living standards

These notes, which relate to AQA specification section 3.4.1, prepare you to answer AQA examination questions on:

- economic growth and the economic cycle
- the costs and benefits of economic growth
- national income and standards of living

Essential information

What you already know about economic growth, the economic cycle and living standards

In your AS course, you came across most of what you need to know for answering ECON 4 exam questions on economic growth and the economic cycle. However, ECON 4 exam questions on these topics may require greater knowledge of the causes and effects of economic growth and cyclical fluctuations, including for example the

role of technical progress in promoting economic growth. The Unit 2 specification at AS makes no mention of living standards, so this is an important 'add on' topic in the Unit 4 specification.

Long-term economic growth

Long-term economic growth can be defined as an increase in the economy's production potential. Figure 2 illustrates two ways of showing long-term economic growth on a diagram. In panel (a) of Figure 2, long-term growth is shown by the outward movement of the **economy's production possibility frontier**, which shifts from PPF_1 to PPF_2. (A rightward movement of the economy's long-run aggregate supply (*LRAS*) curve also illustrates long-term economic growth.) Long-term growth is depicted in panel (b) by the upward-sloping straight line labelled 'Trend output'.

> **Knowledge check 4**
>
> What is a production possibility frontier?

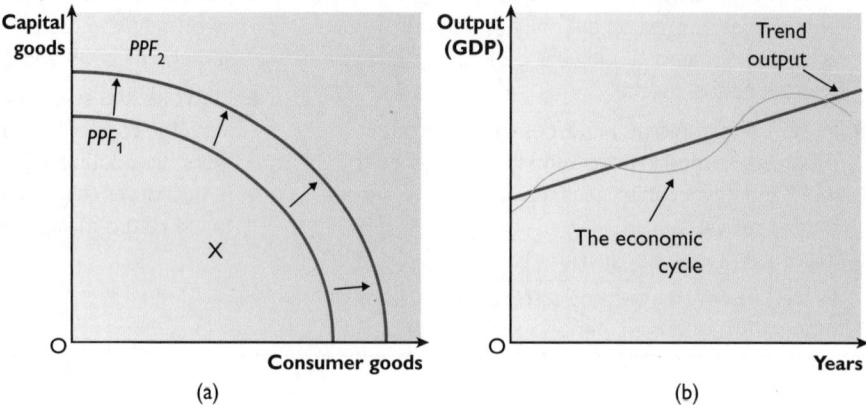

(a)   (b)

Figure 2 Aspects of economic growth

Short-term economic growth

In panel (a) of Figure 2, a movement from a point *inside* the frontier to a point on the frontier illustrates **short-term economic growth** or economic recovery. Short-term growth is also shown by the upward-sloping sections of the 'wavy' line drawn in panel (b). The 'wavy' line illustrates the **economic cycle** (or business cycle) and the actual level of real output at different points in time. Short-term growth occurs in the recovery and boom phases of the economic cycle when real output grows from year to year.

Negative economic growth or economic decline

Until 2008, the UK's trend growth rate was positive at around 2.5% a year. At the time of writing (in autumn 2011), there are fears that the trend growth rate has declined, perhaps falling to close to zero. If trend growth falls to below zero, which is a situation of negative economic growth, the economy's production possibility frontier shifts inwards and the slope of the trend output line in panel (b) changes from positive to negative. By contrast, short-term economic decline would be shown in panel (a) by a movement to a point inside the frontier such as X, and in panel (b) by a downward-sloping section of the 'wavy' line showing the economic cycle.

Negative economic growth This is measured by a fall in real GDP.

Recessions

A recession occurs when short-term economic growth is negative for 6 months (two quarters) or more. (This is the definition of a recession in the UK, though some other countries define recession in different ways.) Prior to 2012, the most recent recession occurred in 2008 and 2009. In 2010 and 2011 growth was so slow that many economists feared the UK economy would soon enter the second 'dip' of a 'double dip' recession. By the time you read this Guide, you will know whether this happened.

Output gaps

When a recession occurs, the actual output line drawn in panel (b) of Figure 2 falls below the trend output line. As a result, the economy experiences a negative 'output gap'. The negative output gap continues during the recovery phase of the economic cycle, but turns into a positive output gap as soon as the actual output line rises above the trend output line. An output gap (negative or positive) measures the difference between the *actual* level of real output and the output that *would* be produced if the economy grew continuously at its trend rate. This is another term you learnt at AS.

A further look at long-term economic growth

Long-term economic growth results from investment in new capital goods (physical capital), which enlarges the national capital stock, and in human beings (human capital). But while investment is an important factor in the growth process, it may not be as important as technical progress. Until quite recently, economists had little to say about the causes of technical progress. However, a relatively new theory, known as **endogenous growth theory**, incorporates the causes of technical progress into the theoretical explanation of the growth process. The theory suggests that governments can create supply-side conditions that favour investment and technical progress. These conditions include external economies for businesses, often in the form of infrastructure, and a favourable entrepreneurial climate which includes a judicial system protecting patents and other intellectual property rights, and which enforces the law of contract.

A further look at short-term economic growth

Whereas successful supply-side policies promote long-term economic growth, short-term economic growth is generally associated with increasing aggregate demand. When the economy is producing at a point inside its production possibility frontier, an increase in aggregate demand is needed to close the resulting negative output gap. Aggregate demand can, of course, be increased by autonomous increases in consumption, investment and/or exports. But given the likelihood that the negative output gap was caused by a collapse of consumer and/or business confidence, or by a reduction in demand for the country's exports, government intervention may be required. Expansionary monetary policy, such as cutting interest rates, and/or expansionary fiscal policy, such as tax cuts, shift the *AD* curve rightward and promote short-term economic growth.

Fluctuations in economic activity

Fluctuations in economic activity occur in three main ways: the economic cycle, seasonal fluctuations and a possible long cycle that lasts perhaps 60 years.

Fluctuations related to the economic cycle

Economic cycles, which are 4–12 years long, are caused primarily by fluctuations in aggregate demand (i.e. by shifts to the left and right of the *AD* curve). There are a number of different theories of the economic cycle and it is advisable to learn at least two theories in some depth. Examples include the following:

- Rapid growth produces a **speculative bubble** in asset prices (e.g. housing and/or shares), which rise far above the assets' real value. The bubble bursts, destroying consumer and/or business confidence. People stop spending and the economy falls into recession..
- The **political business cycle**. UK governments, which are elected about every 5 years, may try to engineer a pre-election boom (to buy votes) and then deflate or contract the economy immediately after the election — until the next pre-election boom.
- Random **demand shocks** (and sometimes **supply shocks**) hit and throw the economy off course.

Seasonal fluctuations

Seasonal fluctuations are related to climate (for example, very cold winters closing down the building trade) and seasonal changes in demand (for example, the approach of Christmas leading to a seasonal shopping spree which boosts consumption).

Long economic cycles

At the opposite extreme to seasonal fluctuations in economic activity, long cycles of about 60 years have been identified. Significant improvements in technical progress (on the supply side of the economy) cause firms to invest in completely new technology, which triggers a long period of boom. Electrification and the automobile have had this effect. Around 2000, many economists believed that information and communication technology (ICT) was having a similar effect, possibly creating a **new economy**. However, the onset of recession in 2008 dampened this enthusiasm. In the past, long booms ran out of steam when the innovating technology became fully used — until, of course, the next burst of technical activity created another boom.

Stabilising the economic cycle

Demand management policies can be used to try to reduce fluctuations in the economic cycle. In the Keynesian era and in 2008/09, fiscal policy was used in this way, but these days monetary policy is generally used to do this. In a boom when the economy is overheating, the Bank of England raises interest rates to contract or deflate aggregate demand. By contrast, in a recession the Bank of England cuts interest rates to reflate or boost aggregate demand. But successful stabilisation requires accurate timing. Bad timing can destabilise the economic cycle and make it more volatile, and by causing long-term risky investments to be abandoned in favour of less risky short-term projects, unexpected interest rate (or tax) changes may affect competitiveness and long-term growth adversely.

The costs and benefits of economic growth

The ultimate purpose of economic activity is to improve economic welfare and people's standards of living. Economic growth can help to achieve this, but only if growth is compatible with economic development. Economic growth, which is *measured by* (though not *defined by*) the annual percentage growth in real national output, can have a number of costs which reduce economic welfare or happiness.

By contrast, **economic development**, which includes the quality and not just the quantity of growth, is measured by:

- a general improvement in living standards that reduces poverty and human suffering
- greater access to resources, such as food and housing, required for basic human needs
- greater access to opportunities for human development (e.g. through education and training)
- environmental sustainability and regeneration, through reduced resource depletion and degradation

Resource depletion occurs when finite resources such as oil are used up, and when soil fertility or fish stocks decline irreversibly. By contrast, resource degradation is best illustrated by pollution of air, water and land. To benefit people in the long run, growth (and development) must be sustainable. **Sustainable economic growth** means the use of:

- renewable rather than non-renewable resources
- technologies that minimise pollution and other forms of resource degradation

Examiner tip
Exam questions are frequently set on the costs or benefits of economic growth, or possibly on the two concepts taken together.

The use and limitations of national income as an indicator of changes in living standards

When using national income figures to measure economic welfare, real national income per capita (or real GDP per capita) should be used to overcome the fact that prices rise and the population changes. Used in this way, national income figures provide quite a good estimate of the first two elements in the standard of living shown below:

$$\begin{array}{l}\text{standard} \\ \text{of living}\end{array} = \begin{array}{l}\text{economic welfare} \\ \text{derived from goods} \\ \text{and services} \\ \text{purchased} \\ \text{in the market} \\ \text{economy}\end{array} + \begin{array}{l}\text{economic welfare} \\ \text{derived from public} \\ \text{goods and merit} \\ \text{goods provided} \\ \text{collectively} \\ \text{by the state}\end{array} + \begin{array}{l}\text{economic welfare} \\ \text{derived from quality} \\ \text{of life factors, external} \\ \text{benefits minus external} \\ \text{costs of intangibles}\end{array}$$

However, national income statistics both underestimate and overestimate economic welfare and living standards for the whole population.

How rising national income statistics underestimate changes in living standards

National income statistics *underestimate* activity because the non-monetised economy (such as housework and DIY) is under-represented, and because activity undertaken illegally in the hidden economy (or black economy) is omitted. The value of positive externalities shown in the third element of standards of living is also omitted from national income statistics. Improvements in the quality of goods may also be under-represented in national income statistics.

Living standards (or standard of living) The level of wealth, comfort and material goods available either to the whole population or to particular groups within the population, including such factors as income, quality and availability of housing, access to health care and the number of days' holiday per year.

How rising national income statistics overestimate changes in living standards

An important reason why national income statistics *overestimate* living standards and welfare relates to negative externalities such as pollution and congestion, and to activities such as crime. What is in effect a welfare loss may be shown as an increase in national output, falsely indicating an apparent welfare gain. For example, the stresses and strains of producing an ever-higher national output lead to a loss of leisure time and make people ill more often. Loss of leisure and poorer health are welfare losses. But in the national accounts, these show up as extra production and as extra consumption of health care, both of which imply a welfare gain. Likewise, installing 'regrettables' such as burglar alarms raises national income, but most people would prefer a crime-free environment and no burglar alarms. Significant disparity in income distribution also reduces the value of national income statistics as a measure of welfare. In developing countries the income distribution is typically extremely unequal and only a small fraction of the population may benefit materially from economic growth.

Comparing national income between countries

Comparisons of national income per head between countries are misleading if the relative importance of the non-monetised economy differs significantly between countries. There are also differences in the degree of statistical sophistication in data collection, particularly between developed and developing countries, and a lack of international uniformity in methods of classifying and categorising national accounts. Further problems occur when making comparisons if different commodities are consumed. For example, expenditure on fuel, clothing and building materials is likely to be greater in developed countries with cold climates than in much warmer developing economies. But we must take care not to deduce from this single fact that greater expenditure — for example, on home heating — indicates higher real income and living standards.

A common method of comparing GDP per capita in different countries is to convert the GDP figures for each country into a common currency such as the US dollar. However, this calculation suffers from the assumption that the exchange rates between local currencies and the dollar are valued correctly, in the sense that a dollar's worth of output in one country becomes immediately and accurately comparable with a dollar's worth of output in any other country. This can never be so. Exchange rate changes only reflect the price changes of internationally traded goods. As there is a much wider gap in developing countries than in developed countries between the price changes of internationally traded and non-traded goods, GNP figures measured in US dollars tend to underestimate real levels of income and output in developing economies. The solution to this problem is to establish **purchasing power parity (PPP) exchange rates**, which means that a PPP dollar, or any PPP currency, buys the same quantity of a good everywhere in the world.

The **United Nations Human Development Index (HDI)** provides a better means of comparing welfare in different countries than national income or GDP statistics. The HDI combines measures of life expectancy, educational attainment and GDP per

Examiner tip

Make sure you familiarise yourself with the meaning of GNP, GDP and GDP per capita.

capita for all the world's countries and measures the economic development of a country rather than just its level of national income.

Examination questions and skills

Examination questions which require detailed explanation of theories of growth are *not* likely to be set. You might, however, be asked to explain the causes of the economic cycle, possibly disguised in a question on the causes of fluctuations in economic activity. Alternatively, questions may centre on the *effects* (rather than the *causes*) of economic growth and/or cycles: for example, focusing on the costs and benefits of economic growth.

Common examination errors

- Measuring economic growth in terms of the growth of nominal output rather than real output.
- Confusing long-term economic growth with economic recovery.
- Confusing a cyclical upturn with the trend rate of economic growth.
- Failing to understand the difference between economic growth and economic development.
- Failing to understand sustainable economic growth, resource depletion and resource degradation.

Examiner tip
An exam question may ask you to evaluate the extent to which GDP figures provide an adequate measure of living standards.

Summary

- Economic growth divides into long-term and short-term economic growth.
- Long-term growth is defined as an increase in an economy's *potential* output.
- Short-term economic growth or economic recovery results from making use of spare capacity and unemployed labour.
- Supply-side economic policies promote long-term growth, whereas an increase in aggregate demand leads to short-term growth.
- Short-term variations in economic growth, positive and negative, relate to the economic cycle or business cycle.

- A recession, defined as 6 months or more of negative growth, occurs in the downturn of the economic cycle.
- A recession is associated with a negative output gap, whereas a positive output gap occurs in a boom.
- Economic growth is not the same as economic development, though it can contribute to economic development.
- The United Nations's Human Development Index (HDI) is a better indicator of living standards than gross domestic product (GDP).

Aggregate demand and aggregate supply

These notes, which relate to AQA specification section 3.4.2, prepare you to answer AQA examination questions on:

- understanding the nature of aggregate demand and aggregate supply
- applying the *AD/AS* model to analyse and evaluate problems and policy

Essential information

What you already know about aggregate demand and aggregate supply

The aggregate demand/aggregate supply (AD/AS) macroeconomic model, which is illustrated in Figure 3, is just as important in Unit 4 as it is in Unit 2. You don't need to learn much more about AD/AS for the Unit 4 exam, but you are required to *apply* the model to explain, analyse and evaluate macroeconomic problems and policy in greater depth than you did when answering AS questions.

As in the AS course, the AD/AS macroeconomic model provides the theoretical framework that you are expected to use to analyse and evaluate economic problems and policy relating to economic growth, inflation and unemployment.

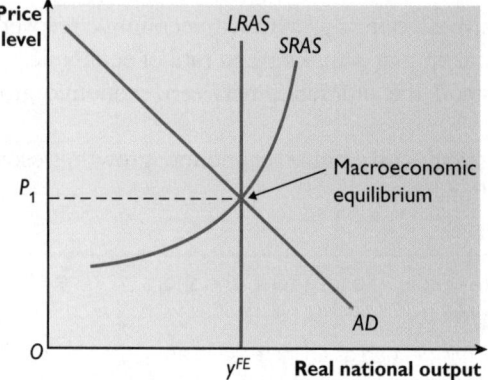

Figure 3 The AD/AS macroeconomic model

The aggregate demand (AD) curve

The **aggregate demand (AD)** curve in Figure 3 shows the total quantities of *real* output that all economic agents — households, firms, the government and the overseas sector — plan to purchase at different domestic price levels, when everything other than the price level is held constant. If any of the components of aggregate demand change, the curve shifts to the right or to the left, depending on the nature of the change. For example, an increase in consumer or business confidence shifts the AD curve to the right, via the effect on consumption or investment. Expansionary monetary and fiscal policies have a similar effect. By contrast, contractionary policy or a collapse in consumer or business confidence causes the AD curve to shift to the left.

The slope of the AD curve

Two factors explain the *slope* of the AD curve, as distinct from a *shift* of the curve. These are:
- A **wealth effect or real balance effect**. Assuming a given *nominal* stock of money (or money supply) in the economy, a decrease in the price level increases people's *real* money balances (i.e. the same amount of money will now buy more). An increase

in real money balances makes people feel wealthier, and since consumption is positively related to wealth, aggregate demand rises as the price level falls.

The second effect follows from this. When the supply of any commodity (in this case, real money balances) increases relative to demand, its price falls. The rate of interest is the price of money; hence an increase in real money balances causes the rate of interest to fall, further stimulating consumption and investment spending.

The aggregate supply (AS) curve

You learnt in the AS course that there are two **aggregate supply (AS)** curves, an upward-sloping **short-run aggregate supply (SRAS)** curve and a vertical **long-run aggregate supply (LRAS)** curve. However, you did not learn much about *why AD* and *AS* curves have the shapes illustrated in Figure 3. The shapes of the curves, particularly the difference between the *SRAS* and the *LRAS* curves, are explained in the next section.

The Keynesian aggregate supply curve

Just as the *AD* curve shows the total quantities of real output that economic agents plan to purchase at different price levels, so the *AS* curve shows the quantities of real output that businesses plan to produce and sell at different price levels.

Panel (a) in Figure 4 shows the inverted L-shaped *AS* curve, based on the Keynesian view of how the economy works, which was prevalent a generation and more ago. Keynesians argued that firms respond to increased demand by increasing output, without requiring an increase in the price level to persuade them to increase output or supply. But when full employment is reached, at real output level y_{FE}, a further increase in aggregate demand (for example, to AD_3) causes prices and not output to rise. Output cannot rise because the economy is producing at full capacity. Excess demand pulls up the price level to P_2 in a **demand-pull inflation**.

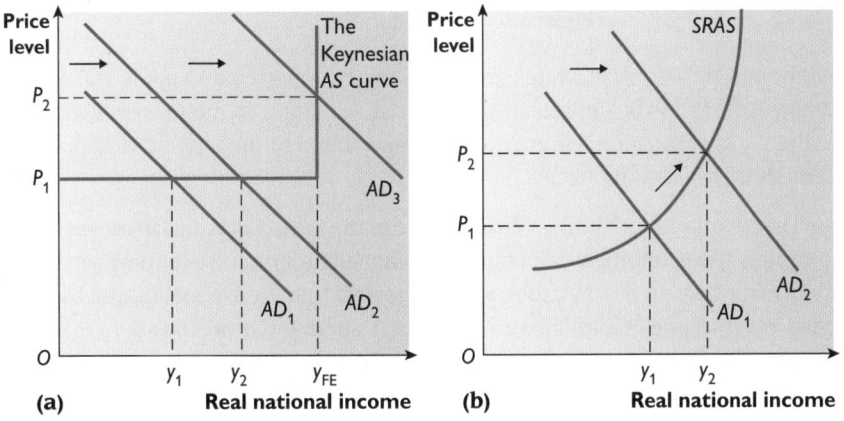

Figure 4 The inverted L-shaped Keynesian *AS* curve and an upward-sloping *SRAS* curve

The upward-sloping short-run aggregate supply (SRAS) curve

Economists now generally reject the inverted L-shaped *AS* curve, believing instead that, in the short run at least, the *AS* curve slopes upwards as depicted in panel (b)

Examiner tip
Exam questions are unlikely to ask you to explain the reasons for the *slope* of the *SRAS* curve. To answer most questions which require *AD/AS* analysis, simply draw an appropriate *AD/AS* diagram, and then get on with the job of shifting the appropriate curve or curves, before explaining the impact of the shift(s) on the issue posed in the question.

of Figure 4. The upward-sloping *SRAS* curve stems from two important elements of microeconomic theory:

- the assumption that firms aim to maximise profit
- the law of diminishing returns (diminishing marginal productivity)

Following an increase in aggregate demand from AD_1 to AD_2 in panel (b), which disturbs an initial macroeconomic equilibrium, the price level must rise to create conditions in which profit-maximising firms are willing to supply more output. To produce more output, more workers must be hired, but as they are hired, their marginal productivity falls and the marginal cost of production rises. When marginal costs rise, the prices charged by firms must also rise, otherwise it is not profitable to produce the extra output. The result is the upward-sloping short-run *AS* curve, which shows that a higher price level is required for firms to supply more output.

The vertical long-run aggregate supply (*LRAS*) curve

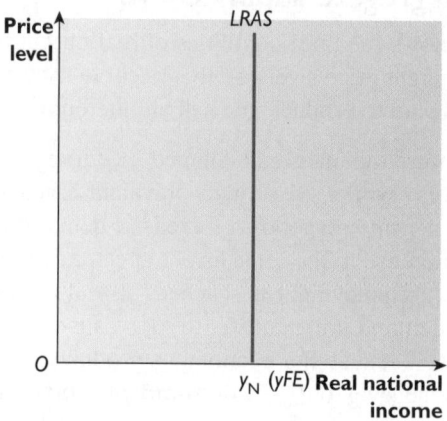

Figure 5 The vertical *LRAS* curve

As mentioned earlier, AQA states that the long-run aggregate supply (*LRAS*) curve should be assumed to be vertical. (Again, this statement is in the AS specification, but not in the A2 specification, where no mention is made of the aggregate supply curve, whether short run or long run.)

The simplest explanation for the vertical slope of the *LRAS* curve lies in the fact that the curve depicts the economy producing at full capacity (or on the economy's production possibility frontier). In this situation it is impossible to increase real output to meet an increase in aggregate demand, so any increase in demand is met by an increase in the price level. The vertical *LRAS* curve shifts to the right if long-run economic growth occurs. Increased capacity allows the economy to produce more output.

Macroeconomic equilibrium The level of output at which $AD = AS$ is also the level of output at which $S + T + M = I + G + X$.

Macroeconomic equilibrium and the economy's natural level of output

You learnt at *AS* that macroeconomic equilibrium occurs at the level of real output at which $AD = AS$. In the short run, this is at the level of output at which the downward-sloping *AD* curve intersects the upward-sloping *SRAS* curve.

In the long run, the equilibrium level of output (which is sometimes called the **natural level of output**) is located at the level of output at which the vertical *LRAS* curve is located. This is labelled y_N in Figure 5. The natural level of output is associated with the natural levels of employment and unemployment of labour in the economy's aggregate labour market.

The *AD/AS* model and economic policy

The *AD/AS* model is particularly useful for analysing the effect of an increase in aggregate demand on the economy because it addresses the important issue of whether expansionary fiscal policy and/or monetary policy will increase real output and jobs (**reflationary**), or whether the price level will increase instead (**inflationary**). In the short run, as has been explained, the answer to this key macroeconomic question depends on the shape of the *SRAS* curve, but in the long run, the vertical slope of the *LRAS* curve means that expanding aggregate demand to a level beyond y_N increases the price level but not real output. According to supply-side economists, this carries the message that the short-run expansionary effect on output and employment, resulting from the government increasing aggregate demand beyond the economy's natural ability to produce additional output, is negated in the long run by the way the supply side of the economy responds to the demand stimulus.

Because supply-side or free-market economists assume that output and employment are at their natural or equilibrium levels, they conclude that it is generally irresponsible for governments to use expansionary fiscal or monetary policy to try to increase national output and employment. While such policies may succeed in the short run, though at the expense of inflation, they are doomed eventually to fail. In the long run, output and employment fall back to their equilibrium or natural levels, which are determined by the economy's production potential or ability to supply. Thus, instead of expanding demand to reduce unemployment *below* its natural rate, free-market economists believe that the government should use microeconomic supply-side policies to reduce the natural rate itself.

If the economy is initially producing *below* y_N, there is a role for increasing aggregate demand to create the demand needed to absorb the economy's ability to supply more goods. However, increasing aggregate demand *beyond* y_N raises prices rather than output.

Examination questions and skills

It is worth emphasising that the aggregate demand/aggregate supply (*AD/AS*) macroeconomic model is unlikely to be mentioned in a Unit 4 examination question, but that, as in the AS course, the model provides the main theoretical framework that you are expected to apply when analysing and evaluating macroeconomic problems and government policies. The *AD/AS* model can be used for analysing economic growth, employment and unemployment, inflation, and both demand-side and supply-side economic policy.

Common examination errors

- Confusing macroeconomic *AD* and *AS* curves with microeconomic demand and supply analysis.

- Mislabelling the axes of *AD/AS* diagrams.
- Confusing *AD/AS* diagrams with Phillips curve diagrams.
- Wasting time deriving *AD* or *AS* curves, instead of applying them to analyse the issue posed by the question.
- Failing to relate *AD/AS* diagrams to demand-side and supply-side economic policy.
- Failing to see the link between the natural level of real output in an *AD/AS* diagram and the natural rate of unemployment in a Phillips curve diagram.

Summary

- The *AD/AS* macroeconomic model is the main theoretical framework you are expected to use when answering questions on the national economy.

- An *AD* curve shows how much real output households, firms, the government and the overseas sector plan to demand at different price levels.

- An *AS* curve shows how much real output producers plan to supply at different price levels.

- A distinction should be made between short-run aggregate supply (*SRAS*) and long-run aggregate supply (*LRAS*).

- Macroeconomic equilibrium occurs at the level of output at which *AD = AS*.

- A distinction can be made between macroeconomic equilibrium in the short run and in the long run.

- The level of output at which long-run macroeconomic equilibrium occurs is also called the natural level of real output.

- The vertical *LRAS* curve is located at the economy's natural level of output.

- *AD/AS* diagrams can be used to illustrate what can happen to real output and the price level when different macroeconomic policies are implemented.

- Expansionary or contractionary fiscal and monetary policies are demand-side policies which shift the *AD* curve to the right or left.

- Supply-side policies aim to shift the *LRAS* curve to the right.

Unemployment and inflation

These notes, which relate to AQA specification section 3.4.1, prepare you to answer AQA examination questions on the causes and consequences of:

- unemployment
- inflation

Essential information

What you already know about unemployment and inflation

Price index A price index is a statistical measure of the average prices of a selected weighted basket of goods, chosen to be representative of all the goods and services in the economy. Changes in the price index are used to measure the rate of inflation.

When studying AS Unit 2: The National Economy, you learnt that there are two measures of unemployment in the UK. These are the **claimant count** and the **Labour Force Survey (LFS)** measure. Likewise, you learnt that the **retail prices index (RPI)** and the **consumer prices index (CPI)** both measure the average price level, and from that the rate of inflation. You also learnt that full employment and unemployment can be illustrated on a production possibility frontier (*PPF*) diagram, and that there are two main causes of inflation: demand inflation (demand-pull) and cost inflation (cost-push).

In panel (a) of Figure 6 (page 27), full employment occurs at all points on the economy's *PPF*, such as *A* and *B*. By contrast, the distance from a point inside the frontier such as

C to the frontier represents unemployment. In panel (b), a shift of aggregate demand to the right pulls up the price level (demand inflation). Panel (b) also illustrates cost-push inflation caused by a shift to the left of aggregate supply.

Who are the unemployed?

There are many people in the UK who are of working age and not working, but who are not 'officially' unemployed. These inactive people of working age include people who stay at home, students without a part-time job and those who retire early. In the early 2000s, the claimant count, which measures those who are unemployed and actually claiming benefit in the form of **jobseeker's allowance**, fell below 1 million, but the LFS measure, which includes the unemployed not claiming benefit, was about half a million higher. However, the onset of recession in 2008 caused unemployment to rise to 2.62 million by September 2011 as measured by the LFS, and to 1.6 million in the same month as measured by the claimant count.

Knowledge check 10
The UK government has recently replaced the RPI with the CPI for the purpose of index-linking public sector pay and pensions. What does this mean and why did the government do this?

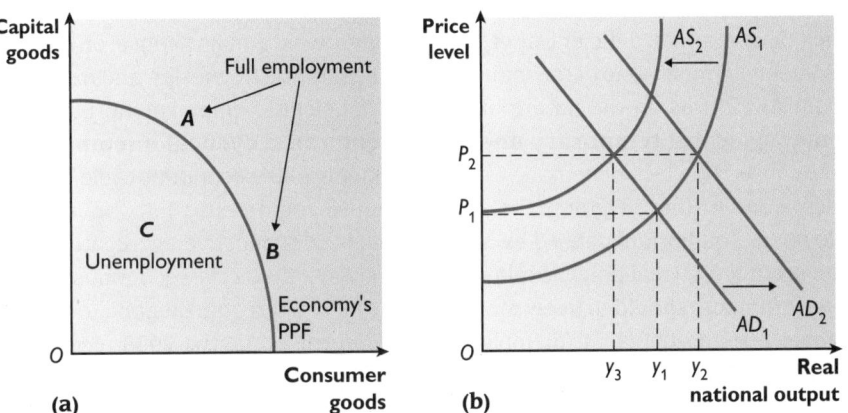

Figure 6 Full employment, unemployment and the causes of inflation

The causes of unemployment

Before Keynes, the **classical** or real-wage **theory of unemployment** (explained on page 11) was the dominant theory of unemployment. Other types or causes of unemployment are **frictional**, **structural** and **demand-deficient**.

Frictional and structural unemployment

In a dynamic economy, change takes place constantly, with some industries declining and others growing. As new products are developed and demand and cost conditions change, firms demand more of some labour skills while the demand for other types of labour declines. Economists use the terms 'frictional unemployment' and 'structural unemployment' to describe the resulting unemployment. Frictional unemployment, as its name suggests, results from frictions in the labour market that create a delay or time-lag during which a worker is unemployed when moving from one job to another. Because there will always be some frictional unemployment, even when there is 'full employment', frictional unemployment is also called **equilibrium unemployment**. Some frictional unemployment can be explained by the search theory of unemployment. Suppose that a worker earning £700 a week in a skilled

Real wage The purchasing power of the nominal or money wage. It represents the goods and services that the money wage can buy.

Knowledge check 11

What is disequilibrium unemployment?

occupation loses her job. There are plenty of vacancies for unskilled workers, at much lower wage rates, but none at £700. In this situation, the worker chooses to remain voluntarily frictionally unemployed, partly because the wage and working conditions do not meet her aspirations, and partly because better-paid vacancies exist which she does not, as yet, know about, but which may be discovered through actively searching the labour market.

Structural unemployment results from the structural decline of industries unable to compete or adapt in the face of either changing demand and new products, or changing ways of producing existing products and the emergence of more efficient competitors in other countries. The growth of international competition has been a particularly important cause of structural unemployment. **Technological unemployment** is a special case of structural unemployment resulting from the successful growth of new industries using labour-saving technology such as automation.

Keynesian or demand-deficient unemployment

Keynes believed that deficient aggregate demand was a major cause of persistent mass unemployment. One of the main disputes separating Keynesian and free-market economists centres on the nature of demand-deficient unemployment. Economists generally agree that **temporary unemployment** (called **cyclical unemployment**) may be caused by a lack of demand in the downswing of the economic cycle. However, Keynes went further, arguing that the economy could settle into an under-full employment equilibrium caused by a continuing lack of effective aggregate demand. As the section on fiscal policy explains (pages 45–47), Keynesian economists believe that governments should actively manage the level of aggregate demand to reduce or eliminate demand-deficient unemployment. In recent years, the 2008 recession led to renewed interest in what Keynes had to say more than 70 years ago about how a lack of aggregate demand may lead to mass unemployment. However, free-market or anti-Keynesian economists and politicians, George Osborne included, continue to dismiss what Keynes had to say.

Examiner tip

Relate the types or causes of unemployment explained above to the natural rate of unemployment explained on page 34 of the Guide.

Knowledge check 12

Explain one *other* consequence of unemployment.

Examiner tip

Make sure you don't confuse the causes and the consequences of both unemployment and inflation.

The consequences of unemployment

Unemployment represents a waste of human capital. Nevertheless, free-market economists believe that a certain amount of unemployment is necessary to make the economy function better. By providing downward pressure on wage rates, unemployment may reduce inflationary pressures. However, it tends to widen income differentials and increase absolute and relative poverty. Higher unemployment means greater spending on unemployment and poverty-related benefits, the opportunity cost of which is less spending on the provision of hospitals, schools and other useful resources.

Can government economic policy reduce unemployment?

Governments generally implement policies to try to reduce unemployment, but the appropriate policy obviously depends on correctly identifying the underlying cause of unemployment. For example, if unemployment is diagnosed in terms of demand deficiency, when the 'true' cause is structural, a policy of fiscal or monetary expansion to stimulate aggregate demand will be ineffective and inappropriate. Indeed, reflation of demand in such circumstances would probably create excess demand, which would raise the price level in a demand-pull inflation, with no lasting beneficial effects on employment.

Examiner tip
At this point you should revise what you learnt at AS about policy conflicts and trading-off between policy objectives.

The free-market or supply-side approach to reducing unemployment

Before the 2008 recession, pro-free-market economists believed that the cause of long-term unemployment in countries such as the UK lay on the supply side of the economy rather than on the demand side. There was much disagreement, however, on the appropriate policies to improve supply-side performance. Free-market economists argued that poor supply-side performance was the legacy of decades of Keynesian interventionism a generation or more ago. They believed that to cut frictional, structural and real-wage unemployment, the economic role of the state should be reduced rather than extended. By setting markets free, encouraging competition and fostering private enterprise and the entrepreneurial spirit, an enterprise culture could be created in which the price mechanism, and not the government, would deliver economic growth and reduce unemployment. In the free-market view, the correct role of government is to create the conditions, through controlling inflation, promoting competitive markets and maintaining the rule of law and social order, in which the market mechanism and private enterprise can function properly.

The Keynesian approach to reducing unemployment

While the pro-free market or supply-side approach remains highly influential, particularly among Conservative politicians, Keynesian economists believe that extremely sluggish recovery following the end of recession in 2009, and the threat of a return to recession (the so-called 'double dip'), mean that deficient aggregate demand continues to be the main cause of UK unemployment. They view unemployment as the result of a massive market failure, which can only be cured by interventionist policies to modify the market and make it function better. Perhaps the truth lies somewhere in the middle. Arguably, recent and current persistent mass unemployment may result from both supply-side and demand-side factors, so both supply-side and demand-side policies should be used in tandem to create new jobs.

The causes of inflation: demand-pull and cost-push inflation

Inflation is defined as a persistent or continuous rise in the price level, or as a fall in the value of money. Demand-pull inflation is caused by excess demand in the economy pulling up the price level.

Monetarism The economic theory that centres on the belief that inflation is always and everywhere a monetary phenomenon. The monetarist theory of inflation is a version of demand-pull inflation, locating the underlying cause of inflation in excessive growth of the money supply.

The monetarist theory of inflation

The **quantity theory of money** (which is at the heart of monetarist economic theory) is the oldest theory of demand-pull inflation. According to the quantity theory, the government creates or condones an expansion of the money supply greater than the increase in real national output. As a result, households and firms hold excess money balances which, when spent, pull up the price level — given the fact that in the short run, real output cannot expand in line with the increase in spending power.

The quantity theory of money can be developed from the **equation of exchange**:

money supply (or stock × velocity of circulation = price × total transactions in
of money) of money level the economy

or: $MV = PT$

For an increase in the money supply (on the left-hand side of the equation) to pull up the price level (on the right-hand side), the velocity of circulation of money (how often money is spent) and total transactions (an indicator of real national income) must both be constant, or at least stable. Keynesians do not accept these monetarist assumptions. As a result, the quantity theory of money and the causes of inflation form another major area of dispute between Keynesian and free-market economists.

The Keynesian version of demand-pull inflation

Arguing that governments condone excessive increases in the money supply, monetarists blame governments for inflation. By contrast, Keynesian theories of demand-pull inflation generally ignore the money supply and locate the cause of inflation in the factors that increase consumer spending and borrowing, and in the tendency of governments to increase public spending and budget deficits (in fiscal policy) in order to win elections.

The Keynesian theory of cost-push inflation

However, many Keynesians favour the cost-push theory of inflation, which can be illustrated by a shift to the left of the short-run *AS* curve. Two variants of cost-push inflation are **wage cost-push inflation** and **import cost-push inflation**.

Until recently, cost-push theory located the cause of inflation in trade union activity and in other causes of market imperfection in both the product market and the labour market. In labour markets, their strength enables trade unions to bargain for money wage increases in excess of any rise in labour productivity. Monopoly firms pay these wage increases, partly because of the costs of disrupting production and partly because they believe that they can pass on the increasing costs as price rises. Cost-push theories usually assume that wages are determined through the process of collective bargaining, while in the goods market, prices are formed by a cost-plus pricing rule through which monopolistic firms add a standard profit margin to their costs when setting prices. Thus trade union militancy and big businesses' monopoly power were blamed for inflation.

In recent years, with the decline of trade union power and militancy, external economic shocks, such as that resulting from a sudden rise in the world prices of oil, food and commodities like copper, have been blamed for triggering cost-push inflation, though arguably the underlying cause of these shocks lies in excess global demand for scarce energy, food and commodities.

The consequences of inflation

Everybody agrees that inflation can have serious adverse effects or costs. However, the seriousness of the adverse effects depends on whether inflation is anticipated or unanticipated. If inflation could be anticipated with complete certainty, it would pose few problems. Households and firms would simply build the expected rate of inflation

Examiner tip
Most recent inflation in the UK has been import cost-push and not demand-pull.

into their economic decisions, which would not be distorted by wrong guesses. When inflation is relatively low, with little variation from year to year, it is easy to anticipate next year's inflation rate. Creeping inflation can be associated with growing markets, healthy profits and a general climate of business optimism, *greasing the wheels* of the economy. Indeed, a low rate of inflation may be a necessary cost of expansionary policies to reduce unemployment. But some free-market economists argue that inflation acts like *sand in the wheels* of the economy, making it less efficient and competitive. If the *sand-in-the-wheels* effect is stronger than the *greasing-the-wheels* effect, the costs of inflation exceed the benefits.

Particular consequences of inflation are as follows:
- **Distributional effects.** Weaker groups in society on fixed incomes lose, while those in strong bargaining positions gain. Also, with rapid inflation, real rates of interest may be negative. In this situation, lenders are really paying borrowers for the doubtful privilege of lending to them, and inflation acts as a hidden tax, redistributing income and wealth from lenders to borrowers.
- **Distortion of normal economic behaviour.** Inflation can distort consumer behaviour by causing households to bring forward purchases and hoard goods if they expect the rate of inflation to accelerate. Similarly, firms may divert funds out of productive investment in fixed investment projects into unproductive commodity hoarding and speculation.
- **Breakdown in the functions of money.** In a severe inflation, money becomes less useful and efficient as a medium of exchange and store of value. Rapidly changing prices also erode money's functions as a unit of account and standard of deferred payment. In a hyperinflation, less efficient barter replaces the use of money and imposes extra costs on most transactions.
- **International uncompetitiveness.** When inflation is higher than in competitor countries, exports increase in price, putting pressure on a fixed exchange rate. With a floating exchange rate, the exchange rate falls to restore competitiveness, but rising import prices may fuel a further bout of inflation.
- **Shoe leather and menu costs.** Consumers incur shoe leather costs, spending time and effort shopping around and checking which prices have or have not risen. By contrast, menu costs are incurred by firms, which have to adjust price lists more often.

Knowledge check 13

Relate shoe leather costs to information problems that economists often identify.

Examination questions and skills

Examination questions are likely to cover the causes of unemployment and inflation, interrelationships between the two (see the next section), and application of *AD/AS* theory to explain the causes of unemployment and inflation, the costs and benefits of inflation, and how economic policy might reduce unemployment or inflation.

In recent years, particularly in the 2008/09 recession, the fear of deflation (continuously *falling* prices) replaced to some extent the fear of inflation and continuously *rising* prices. (For a few months, deflation did take place during the recession.) Examination questions might continue to reflect the possibility of the return of deflation, though rising prices of energy, food and commodities imported from the rest of the world make this unlikely. Stagflation may be much more likely, and may indeed already be with us.

Common examination errors

- Assuming that full employment means that everybody is employed.
- Failing to understand the difference between and the adequacy of the two ways of measuring unemployment.
- Confusing frictional and structural unemployment.
- Writing about relatively trivial causes of unemployment, such as seasonal and casual unemployment, when the question is about the more important frictional, structural and demand-deficient causes.
- Confusing inflation with a one-off price change, or with relative price changes.
- Failing to appreciate conflicts between full employment and price stability as macroeconomic policy objectives (see the next topic).
- Assuming that inflation is always bad and never good, and that therefore deflation must be good because inflation is bad.
- Failing to understand how price indices such as the CPI measure inflation.

Summary

- The rate of inflation, which is defined as a persistent increase in the average price level, is measured by the consumer prices index and by the retail prices index.
- Total unemployment is measured by the Labour Force Survey method and by the claimant count.
- The rate of CPI inflation is generally higher than the rate of RPI inflation, and LFS unemployment is higher than claimant count unemployment.
- Types of unemployment include frictional, structural and cyclical (demand-deficient or Keynesian) unemployment, all of which figure in the AS specification, together with classical or real-wage unemployment.

- Inflation is caused by both demand-pull and cost-push factors.
- Demand-pull inflation is explained in two different ways, through both monetarist and Keynesian theory.
- Wage cost-push inflation in the UK has been replaced in recent years by import cost-push inflation.
- It is important to distinguish between the causes and the effects of both unemployment and inflation.
- Except when the rate of inflation is low and stable, the costs of inflation are generally assumed to exceed the benefits of inflation.
- Unemployment is bad because it involves a waste of resources.

The Phillips curve and the natural rate of unemployment

These notes, which relate to AQA specification section 3.4.1, prepare you to answer AQA examination questions on:

- the short-run and the long-run Phillips curve
- factors determining the natural rate of unemployment (NRU)
- the implications of the Phillips curve and the NRU for economic policy

Essential information

What you already know about the Phillips curve and the natural rate of unemployment

At AS, you learnt about the conflict between full employment and controlling inflation, as macroeconomic policy objectives. However, the Unit 2 specification makes no mention of the Phillips curve or of the natural rate of unemployment.

The original (short-run) Phillips curve

At the height of the Keynesian era, two or more generations ago in the 1950s, A. W. Phillips argued that a stable inverse statistical relationship exists between the rate of *wage* inflation and the percentage of the labour force unemployed. (More usually these days, the Phillips curve measures the inverse relationship between unemployment and the rate of *price* inflation.)

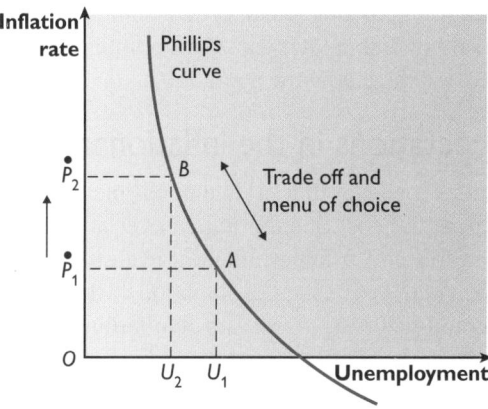

Figure 7 The short-run Phillips curve

The Phillips curve and demand-pull and cost-push inflation

The Phillips curve is *not* a theory of inflation, but it gives support to both the main theories of inflation. In the demand-pull theory, falling unemployment is associated with **excess aggregate demand**, which pulls up wages and prices. In the cost-push theory, falling unemployment increases the market power of workers in the labour market, enabling them to push for higher wages.

The short-run Phillips curve and macroeconomic policy

Although the Phillips curve illustrates the conflict between full employment and control of inflation as policy objectives, it also suggests how the conflict can be dealt with. Suppose that in Figure 7 unemployment is initially U_1 and the rate of inflation is $\dot{P}_1$, with the economy at point A on the Phillips curve. By increasing aggregate demand, the government can move the economy to point B. Unemployment falls to U_2, but at the cost of a higher rate of inflation at $\dot{P}_2$.

Knowledge check 14
Briefly explain a conflict between macroeconomic policy objectives other than the conflict between reducing the rate of inflation and achieving low unemployment.

Knowledge check 15
What are the two main causes of cost-push inflation?

Excess aggregate demand This occurs when the total planned spending of households, firms, and the government and overseas sector exceeds the full employment level of real output in the economy.

Demand management policies Fiscal policy and monetary policy used in a demand-side way to control the level of aggregate demand in the economy.

Examiner tip

Make sure you understand the difference between the *SRPC* and the *LRPC* and don't introduce the 'wrong' curve into your answer to an exam question. Likewise don't confuse Phillips curve diagrams with *AD/AS* diagrams.

Knowledge check 16

Relate the natural rate of unemployment to the equilibrium level of unemployment.

The breakdown of the Phillips relationship

The Phillips curve indicates that by using **demand management policies**, governments can trade off between the number of jobs in the economy and the rate of inflation. Points such as *A* and *B* on the short-run Phillips curve represent a menu of choice from which governments can choose when deciding an acceptable combination of unemployment and inflation. But in the stagflation of the 1970s, accelerating inflation and growing unemployment occurred together. The breakdown of the Phillips curve relationship was a major cause of the free-market counter-revolution that replaced Keynesianism.

The long-run Phillips curve (*LRPC*) and the natural rate of unemployment (NRU)

Economists now generally recognise that the Phillips curve in Figure 7 is a short-run Phillips curve (*SRPC*), representing the *short-run* relationship between inflation and unemployment. In Figure 8(a), a vertical long-run Phillips curve (*LRPC*) has been added to the diagram, cutting the short-run Phillips curve where the rate of inflation is zero. The rate of unemployment at this point is called the **natural rate of unemployment (NRU)**, depicted by the symbol U_N.

The role of expectations in the inflationary process

Free-market economists believe that it is impossible to reduce unemployment below the NRU, except at the cost of suffering an ever-accelerating inflation, which, by eventually accelerating into a hyperinflation, eventually destroys the economy. They argue that the original, Keynesian, explanation of the (short-run) Phillips curve wrongly took into account only the *current* rate of inflation, and ignored the important influence of the *expected* rate of inflation. Figure 8(b) shows what happens when the **role of expectations** is brought into the Phillips curve diagram.

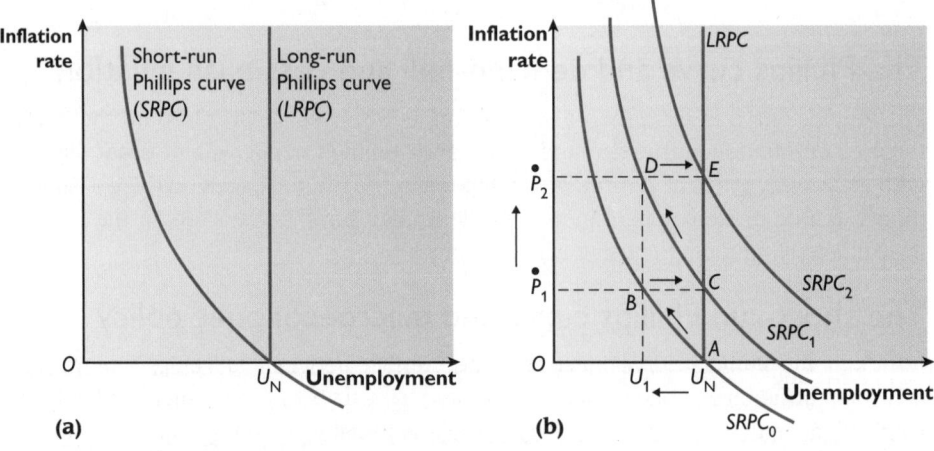

Figure 8 The long-run Phillips curve and the natural rate of unemployment

Let us assume that the rate of growth of labour productivity is zero and that the rate of *price* inflation equals the rate of *wage* inflation. The economy is initially at point

AQA A2 Economics

A, with unemployment at the natural rate U_N. At point A, the rate of inflation is zero, as is the rate of increase of money wages. Let us also assume that people form their expectations of *future* inflation in the next time period solely on the basis of the *current* rate of inflation. At point A, current inflation is zero, so workers expect the future rate of inflation also to be zero.

Suppose the government increases aggregate demand, to trade off along Phillips curve $SRPC_0$ to a point such as B, where unemployment at U_1 is below the natural rate, U_N. Inflation initially rises to $\dot{P}_1$ or 5%. But a point such as B is unsustainable. This is because, for workers to supply more labour, the real wage must rise, yet a rising real wage causes employers to demand less labour. In the short run, more workers may indeed enter the labour market in the false belief that a 5% increase in *money* wages is also a *real* wage increase. This is called money illusion. Similarly, firms may be willing to employ more labour if they also suffer money illusion, believing falsely that rising prices mean that sales revenues are rising faster than labour costs.

How changing expectations shift the short-run Phillips curve

To sustain an increase in employment *above* the natural rate (and to reduce unemployment *below* the NRU), workers and employers must suffer permanent money illusion in equal but opposite directions to keep expectations of inflation, formed in the previous time period, consistently below the actual rate to which inflation has risen. But workers continuously adjust their expectations of future inflation to the rising actual rate and bargain for ever-higher money wages to restore the real wage to the level necessary to reduce unemployment below U_N. As they do this, the short-run Phillips curve shifts outwards from $SRPC_0$ to $SRPC_1$ and so on. There is a separate short-run Phillips curve for each expected rate of inflation. Further out short-run Phillips curves such as $SRPC_1$ and $SRPC_2$ are associated with higher expected rates of future inflation. Conversely, the short-run Phillips curve shifts inwards when the expected rate of inflation falls.

Reducing unemployment below the NRU

Free-market economists argue that, in the long run, the only way to keep unemployment *below* the NRU is to permit the money supply to increase so as to finance an ever-accelerating inflation. For this to happen, inflation has to accelerate above the rate that workers and firms are expecting: for example, from $\dot{P}_1$ to $\dot{P}_2$. But, as noted earlier, an accelerating inflation will eventually create a hyperinflation, which, in the resulting breakdown of economic activity, will almost certainly increase the NRU. Any attempt to reduce unemployment below the NRU is therefore foolhardy and irresponsible. In the short run it accelerates inflation, while in the long run it perversely increases the NRU to an unnecessarily high level.

Stabilising the level of unemployment at the NRU

If the government realises that it made a mistake initially when expanding the economy to point B, it can stabilise the rate of inflation at 5%. Workers and employers see through their earlier money illusion and realise that they have confused money quantities with real quantities. They refuse respectively to supply, and to demand, the labour necessary to keep unemployment below the NRU. The economy then

Money illusion Occurs in times of high and variable inflation, when people confuse changes in the nominal values of economic variables with their real values. Households falsely believe that real rates of interest are positive when in fact they are negative. Workers falsely believe that money wages are rising when in fact they are falling.

Examiner tip
Again, analysis of the role of expectations in the inflationary process is difficult, so think carefully about your choice of exam question.

moves to point C in Figure 8(b). Once point C is reached, any further increase in aggregate demand would move the economy to point D and an inflation rate of $\dot{P}_2$ — and to a repeat of the process just described, but starting from a higher initial rate of inflation.

The theory of adaptive expectations

The theory just described is based on the **theory of adaptive expectations**, in which workers and firms form expectations of what will happen in the *future* only on the basis of what is happening *currently* and upon what has happened in the *recent* past.

The theory of rational expectations

However, new-classical economists favour an alternative theory of how expectations are formed, called the **theory of rational expectations**. According to this theory, it is unrealistic to assume that workers and firms, acting rationally in their self-interest, form expectations of future inflation *solely* on the basis of current or recent inflation. If they can forecast the results of events taking place in the economy now, self-interest dictates that they should quickly modify their economic behaviour to take account of the most up-to-date information available. New-classical economists reject the idea that economic agents suffer money illusion for quite long periods — a vital component in the explanation of the short-run Phillips curve. If expectations are formed *rationally* rather than *adaptively*, any attempt by a government to reduce unemployment below its natural rate by increasing aggregate demand fails, leading solely to accelerating inflation.

Examiner tip

For the most part, adaptive expectations theory is easier to apply in an ECON 4 answer than rational expectations theory.

Supply-side policy and the natural rate of unemployment

Free-market economists of the new-classical or rational expectations school argue that the correct way to reduce unemployment is to reduce the natural level itself, rather than to expand demand to try to reduce unemployment below the NRU. To do this, the government should use appropriate free-market supply-side policies.

Figure 9 shows how supply-side policy, in the form of business and income tax cuts, can shift the long-run Phillips curve to the left and reduce the NRU. A cut in business taxation reduces costs of production, thereby shifting the aggregate demand curve for labour (shown in panel (a)) from AD_{L1} to AD_{L2}. Likewise, income tax cuts granted to workers shift the aggregate supply curve of labour from AS_{L1} to AS_{L2}. As a result, the natural level of *employment* in the aggregate labour market increases from E_{N1} to E_{N2}. This in turn reduces frictional unemployment (and the NRU) in panel (b) of the diagram, shifting the long-run Phillips curve to the left from $LRPC_1$ to $LRPC_2$. The NRU thus falls from U_{N1} to U_{N2}.

Examination questions and skills

Whereas an AS question is likely to ask about the *causes* of unemployment and inflation, an A2 question could also test understanding of the *conflicts* and *trade-offs* between full employment and control of inflation. Questions may or may not

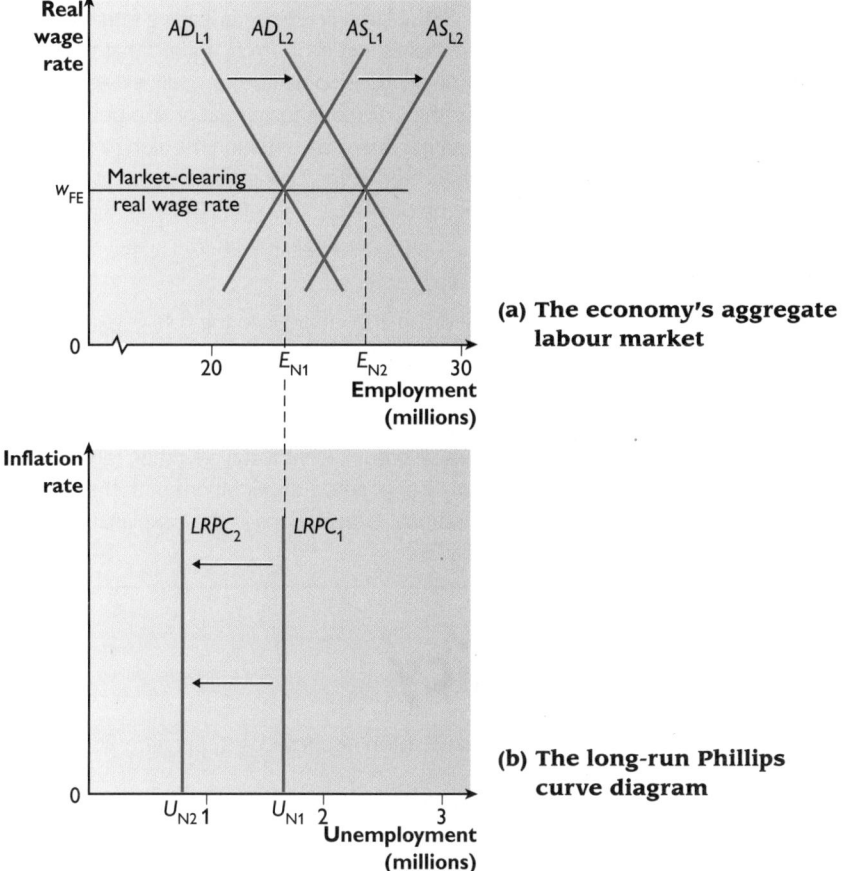

Figure 9 Supply-side policies increasing the natural level of employment and reducing the natural level of unemployment

Knowledge check 17

What is the difference between the natural *rate* of unemployment and the natural *level* of unemployment?

mention the Phillips curve explicitly. In the latter case, you could apply Phillips curve analysis to address the issue or issues posed by the question. Likewise, the natural rate of unemployment is a key analytical concept that may or may not be mentioned in a question. It is important to use the NRU when explaining and evaluating the significance of both demand-side and supply-side economic policies.

Common examination errors

- Confusing short-run and long-run Phillips curves.
- Confusing Phillips curve diagrams with *AD/AS* diagrams.
- Confusing a reduction of unemployment *below* the NRU with a *shift to the left* of the NRU.
- Failing to relate the NRU to the analysis of supply-side economic policy.
- Failing to relate NRU analysis to the functioning of the aggregate labour market.

Examiner tip
The Phillips curve has not yet been mentioned in an examination question, and the NRU has been mentioned only once. While short-run Phillips curve analysis is generally straightforward, introducing analysis of the long-term Phillips curve into an A2 answer often leads to theoretical mistakes and on occasion to irrelevance.

Summary

- The Phillips curve, named after the Keynesian economist A. W. Phillips, is a statistical relationship showing an inverse or negative relationship between the rate of price inflation and the level of unemployment.
- In the second half of the Keynesian era, from the mid-1950s to the early 1970s, Keynesian economists used the Phillips curve to support their theories of inflation, the Keynesian demand-pull theory and the cost-push theory.
- The Phillips curve was not itself a theory of inflation.
- In the 1970s, and perhaps earlier, the Phillips relationship broke down when accelerating inflation and growing unemployment occurred together.
- The 'death' of the Phillips curve was associated with the crisis in Keynesian economics and the free-market revival.
- In 1968, Milton Friedman, a leading free-market and monetarist economist, argued that the Phillips curve relationship had never really existed and that the 'true' long-term relationship between unemployment and inflation lies along a vertical line located at the economy's natural rate of unemployment.
- The vertical line became known as the long-run Phillips curve.
- Friedman also introduced the role of expectations into his explanation of inflation, in the form of the theory of adaptive expectations.
- A later group of free-market economists, the new-classical school, went a stage further, replacing the theory of adaptive expectations with the theory of rational expectations in their explanation of inflation.

Monetary policy

These notes, which relate to AQA specification section 3.4.2, prepare you to answer AQA examination questions on the:

- instruments and objectives of monetary policy
- role of the Bank of England in implementing monetary policy in the UK
- link between financial markets and monetary policy

Essential information

What you already know about monetary policy

In your AS course, you learnt that monetary policy attempts to achieve the policy objectives set by the government using monetary instruments such as interest rates and controls on bank lending. You also learnt that the Bank of England, the country's central bank, raises or lowers interest rates, and that this shifts the *AD* curve to the left or to the right in the *AD/AS* macroeconomic model, thereby affecting output, employment and the rate of inflation.

What is money?

Money is best defined by the two main functions it performs in the economy, as a **medium of exchange** and as a **store of value** or **wealth**. **Cash** and **bank deposits** are the two main forms of money. Cash is really just the small change of the monetary system. Bank deposits, which are liabilities of the private enterprise banking system, are by far the major part of modern money.

Examiner tip
Make sure you don't confuse monetary policy with fiscal policy. The two policies can be used to support and reinforce each other, or they can be used to pursue different policy objectives.

Knowledge check 18
What is a bank deposit?

Interest rates and monetary policy

For the most part, monetary policy has centred on the Bank of England raising or lowering its own interest rate, or indeed keeping it stable (e.g. at 0.5%), to control or influence the ability of the commercial banks to create deposits when they lend to customers.

The Bank of England's interest rate is called **Bank Rate**. In theory, a change in Bank Rate affects the rates of interest charged to borrowers and paid to savers by financial institutions such as banks and building societies. Changes in Bank Rate affect other interest rates partly through an 'announcement effect', and partly through the Bank of England's intervention in financial markets, which massages other short-term interest rates in the direction of the official rate.

Interest rate The price paid to borrow money or the reward for lending money.

The limitations of interest rate policy

Before 2009, UK monetary policy focused almost solely on interest rate policy. However, the 2008 recession showed the limitations of cutting Bank Rate in order to stimulate aggregate demand to draw the economy out of recession. Bank Rate cannot be cut below zero, and because it had already been cut to the extremely low rate of 0.5%, there was virtually no scope for further cuts in Bank Rate to boost aggregate demand.

Quantitative easing

In 2009, the ineffectiveness of interest rate policy in dealing with the problem of recession led to the introduction of a 'new' monetary policy instrument to stimulate aggregate demand. The instrument is called **quantitative easing (QE)**.

The background to QE

To understand QE, you must remember the point made earlier that bank deposits, rather than cash, form by far the largest part of money. Banks can only lend new money to customers if they possess capital assets to 'back' the new loans. But the **credit crunch**, which in 2007 preceded and was a cause of the 2008 recession, stemmed from 'greedy' banks lending too much money, unbacked by sufficient capital, to their customers. (The most risky of these loans to house buyers were called **sub-prime mortgages**.) In order to restore the amount of capital they possessed as a ratio of their loans, the banks drastically reduced the amount they were prepared to lend to their customers and asked for early repayment of existing loans. They also cut the overdraft facilities of existing customers, many of which were small businesses. By worsening the credit crunch, this made the recession deeper and prevented recovery from recession.

Knowledge check 19

What was the credit crunch?

The introduction of QE

In 2009, the Bank of England responded to this situation by starting the policy of quantitative easing. Much of the capital held by high street banks to back their loans to customers takes the form of UK government bonds (gilt-edged securities or gilts) purchased by the banks on the bond market. With QE, the Bank of England buys these illiquid bonds from the banks, paying for them with the liquid 'new money'

that QE creates. (This is often described as 'printing new money', but this is a rather misleading description of quantitative easing. The new money created by QE is electronic money rather than paper money.) Between 2009 and 2010, when the policy was temporarily suspended, £200 billion of new money was injected into the banking system by QE.

QE's basic problem

In 2009 the Bank of England and the government hoped that, being awash with cash, high street banks would lend more to the general public to get the economy out of recession. The general public would spend the new money, aggregate demand would increase and the economy would recover from recession. However, this did not happen. The reason for this stems from the fact that, before QE started, the banks were already short of liquid capital assets. This meant that, instead of lending the £200 billion to their customers, the banks simply 'sat on the money'. Rather than quickly passing the money on for their customers to spend, the banks used much of the £200 billion to restore the amount of liquid capital they owned. Because of its relative ineffectiveness, quantitative easing was suspended in 2010.

QE1 and QE2

By late 2011, the danger of entering the second 'dip' of a 'double dip' recession meant that many British economists were calling for a second bout of quantitative easing in the UK. This duly happened in October 2011 when the Bank of England announced the reintroduction of quantitative easing, releasing a further £75 billion of new money into the banking system. The earlier phase of quantitative easing has been called QE1; the second phase is QE2. Even more new money may eventually be released.

Monetarism

For a fairly short period from the late 1970s until the mid-1980s, UK monetary policy was **monetarist**. Monetarists are so called because they believe that inflation is caused by prior excess growth of the money supply, via the **quantity theory of money**. They also believe, first, that control of inflation should be the government's main policy objective and, second, that to control inflation the rate of growth of the money supply must be strictly controlled. In the short-lived monetarist experiment, monetarist policies did not work, and UK monetary policy ceased to be monetarist after the mid-1980s. However, two important features of monetarist monetary policy have survived. First, monetarists disliked unnecessary government intervention in the economy and therefore abandoned the controls on bank lending used by the Keynesians. Second, control of inflation has continued to be the ultimate objective of UK monetary policy, though this was not very evident in 2010 and 2011.

The framework of UK monetary policy

The framework of current UK monetary policy was created by a Conservative government in 1992, modified by the incoming Labour government in 1997, and given a few minor changes when the decision was made not to replace the pound with the euro in 2003. Before 1997, the monetary authorities who implemented monetary policy were the Chancellor of the Exchequer (in charge of the Treasury) and the Governor of the Bank of England. The authorities raised or lowered interest rates to

Examiner tip

Before 2010, quantitative easing was not included in the AQA specification. Quantitative easing was introduced into the Unit 4 specification in 2010, so A2 exam questions may now mention it. Prior to 2010 a good answer to a question on monetary policy might show knowledge of the concept. Since 2010, you may be *required* to display such knowledge.

Knowledge check 20

What would be the main element of a monetarist monetary policy?

Examiner tip

Many students wrongly believe that monetarism and monetary policy are exactly the same. Monetarism is a body of economic theory that explains inflation in terms of a prior increase in the money supply. As the answer to Knowledge check 20 explains, monetary policy can be monetarist, though in recent decades this has not really been the case.

try to keep the inflation rate below a target rate set by the government. The policy had a **deflationary bias**, since the further inflation fell below the target rate, the greater the deemed success of monetary policy.

In 1997, the Labour government reformed the monetary policy framework, primarily by making the Bank of England operationally independent in implementing policy to hit the inflation rate target set by the government, and by establishing the **Monetary Policy Committee (MPC)** to formulate and undertake policy to achieve this goal.

The inflation rate target of monetary policy

Monetary policy is implemented in the UK so as to 'hit' the **inflation rate target** set by the government. This is 2.0% inflation measured by changes in the consumer prices index (CPI). Prior to the election of a Labour government in May 1997, monetary policy aimed to get the inflation rate on or below the target rate set by the government. In 1997 this changed. The MPC is now prepared to reduce interest rates to stimulate output and employment if it believes that, on unchanged policies, an inflation rate below the target rate will be accompanied by an undesirable fall in output and employment. In the government's words: 'the primary objective of monetary policy is price stability, but subject to that, the Bank of England must also support the government's economic policy objectives, including those for growth and employment'.

The pre-emptive nature of monetary policy

In theory, though not always in practice, UK monetary policy is **pre-emptive**. Policy-makers at the Bank of England estimate what the inflation rate is likely to be 18 months to 2 years ahead (the medium term) if policy (that is, interest rates) remains unchanged. If the forecast rate of inflation is too far away from the target rate set by the government, the Bank is prepared to change interest rates immediately to prevent the forecast inflation rate becoming a reality. The Bank is also prepared to raise or lower interest rates to pre-empt any likely adverse effects on the inflation rate of an outside shock hitting the economy. Such a shock can justify a sudden change in interest rates to meet the unforeseen danger caused by the shock.

Economic 'shocks' and UK monetary policy

For many months, prior to 2012 at least, the UK rate of inflation was well above the 2% CPI target set by the government. According to the monetary policy framework, the Bank of England should have raised Bank Rate well above 0.5% in order to bring down the rate of inflation. This has not happened. Some economists believe that the Bank of England has merely been giving 'lip service' to the 2% CPI inflation rate target. The Bank's response is to say that the effect of adverse shocks drops out of the measurement of the inflation rate after 12 months. Unless further unexpected shocks hit the economy, the inflation rate will fall towards 2% in 2012.

Economic shock An event which produces a significant unexpected change in the economy, often caused by events outside the economy. An economic shock may be benign or malign, and on the demand or supply side of the economy.

The first of two major economic shocks that have thrown monetary policy off course consists of recession itself, very slow and weak recovery from recession and the threat of a 'double dip'. The second shock has been cost-push inflation imported from the rest of the world.

Slow and weak recovery from recession

Given the fact (explained in the next topic) that fiscal policy has recently been highly contractionary, the UK government has persuaded the Bank of England to adopt an extremely loose monetary policy centring on extremely low interest rates to try to raise the rate of economic growth. However, as explained earlier, low interest rates have not been very effective in boosting economic growth.

Import cost-push inflation

Conventional monetary policy, which focuses on managing aggregate demand, is generally ineffective in reducing import cost-push inflation caused by rising energy, food and commodity prices. Indeed, by causing the exchange rate to fall, low interest rates increase cost-push inflation through the raising of import prices.

Evaluating the success of UK monetary policy

Before 2008

Before the 2008 recession and the introduction of quantitative easing in 2009, the success of UK monetary policy was measured by the extent to which the inflation rate target set by the government had been met as a result of interest rates set by the Bank of England. Judged in this way, monetary policy was generally extremely successful. The rate of inflation measured by the CPI almost always lay between 1% above and below the 2% target. Whether this success was the result of the wisdom of the MPC or the result of benign global economic conditions (e.g. falling commodity prices) is a matter of some debate.

After 2008

Just before the onset of recession in 2008, a burst of cost-push inflation caused by rapidly rising oil and commodity prices meant that inflation temporarily breached the 3% ceiling rate. However, for a few months this was quickly followed by the inflation rate falling and indeed becoming negative (deflation), when measured against changes in the RPI. By 2008, events in the outside world had changed for the worse. Not only did the UK 'import' recession from the USA, but as a result of rising oil, food and commodity prices, the UK once again began to 'import' cost-push inflation from the rest of the world. The rate of CPI inflation rose again well above the target rate of 2% and the ceiling rate of 3%. By October 2011, the rates of RPI and CPI inflation were at three-year highs of 5.6% and 5.2% respectively – the latter over 3% above the CPI target rate set by the government.

Thus, between 2008 and 2011, the Bank of England was clearly unsuccessful in hitting the inflation rate target. Monetary policy was being aimed not at reducing inflation, but at stimulating aggregate demand in an attempt to boost recovery from recession. The ongoing failure to bring inflation down and the fact that low interest rates had little effect on aggregate demand meant that monetary policy was no longer successful in achieving its objective(s). As mentioned earlier, the 2% inflation rate appeared to lack credibility. Many economists were arguing that the framework within which monetary policy operates needs radical change.

Evaluating quantitative easing

Supporters of QE1 believe that although it failed to lead to a rapid demand-led recovery from recession, by increasing the money supply QE1 had the effect of preventing the recession deepening into a full-blown depression.

By contrast, critics of quantitative easing claim that this benefit, if it occurred, has been countered by the far greater danger of an increase in the money supply adding to the already high rate of inflation. QE is equivalent to the Bank of England pouring petrol on the fire of commodity price inflation over which the Bank has no control.

Critics also argue that despite their protestations, the Bank of England and the government may cynically be quite relaxed about a high inflation rate, since it reduces the real value of government debt (the National Debt).

And although QE2 is even less likely than QE1 to increase aggregate demand significantly, indirectly it does so by causing the pound's exchange rate to fall, thereby increasing the price competitiveness of British exports.

Finally, by increasing the price of government bonds, QE has greatly reduced the effective rate of interest earned by savers with investments in gilt-edged securities. This in turn has reduced to a pittance the income earned by people reaching retirement age whose private pensions are based on gilt yields. Although young people with mortgages continue to benefit significantly from low interest rates, QE has eroded the incomes received by many private pensioners.

Money and financial markets

Everyone, except the destitute, makes decisions on the form of asset in which to keep wealth (an asset is anything that has value). First, people choose between physical assets such as houses (which provide a good hedge against inflation) and financial assets. Second, they choose the form of financial asset to hold. Financial assets vary in terms of their liquidity and profitability. Liquidity measures the ease with which an asset can be converted into money and the certainty of what it will be worth when converted into money. Providing it is acceptable and can be used as a means of payment, money is the most liquid of all assets. However, in contrast to less liquid assets such as shares and government bonds (gilt-edged securities), money earns little or no interest.

Financial market A market in which financial assets (e.g. currencies, government debt and shares) are traded, as distinct from other markets such as goods markets and labour markets.

Examiner tip
The Unit 4 specification does not require students to possess knowledge of the main financial markets in the UK. However, to understand properly both monetary policy and fiscal policy, it is useful to possess some knowledge of how financial markets operate.

Shares and gilts, which are generally more profitable than money, are also marketable – they can be sold second hand on the stock exchange. The stock exchange is part of the capital market on which public companies (plcs) sell new issues of shares to raise long-term capital, and on which the government sells new issues of government bonds (gilt-edged securities or 'gilts') to finance its budget deficit (in fiscal policy).

Examination questions and skills

You should expect two main types of examination question on monetary policy. The first type mentions monetary policy explicitly, asking perhaps for an evaluation of its success, or for a comparison of monetary and fiscal policy. The second type of question is more general, requiring, for example, an evaluation of economic policy in stabilising the economic cycle. Monetary policy is not mentioned in the question, but

a good answer would explain, analyse and evaluate how monetary policy (and also fiscal policy) might be used to control the level of aggregate demand in the economy. Monetary policy is a form of demand-side policy. Monetary policy is *not* a supply-side policy, though students sometimes wrongly argue that controlling the money supply is an example of supply-side policy.

Common examination errors

- Assuming that modern monetary policy is monetarist.
- Confusing monetary policy with fiscal policy.
- Confusing monetary policy instruments such as the interest rate with the policy objective of controlling inflation.
- Failing to realise that bank deposits are the main form of modern money.
- Failing to understand that interest rate policy may become ineffective as inflation approaches zero.
- A lack of appreciation of the links between monetary policy and the exchange rate.
- Misunderstanding the way quantitative easing works.

- Money is defined by its medium of exchange and store of value functions.
- Cash and bank deposits are the two main forms of money, with the latter the more important.
- Monetary policy is the part of macroeconomic policy which uses policy instruments such as interest rates and quantitative easing (QE) to achieve objectives such as the control of inflation.
- As bank deposits are the main form of money, to be successful, monetary policy must aim to control the rate of growth of bank deposits.
- The rate of interest has generally been by far the most important monetary policy instrument, though recently quantitative easing has temporarily been used.
- The UK government sets monetary policy targets, but the Monetary Policy Committee (MPC) at the Bank of England implements monetary policy.

- Since the 1990s, the rate of inflation has been the main monetary policy objective.
- Currently, monetary policy aims to hit a 2% inflation rate target, measured in terms of changes in the consumer prices index (CPI).
- Since the 2008/09 recession, achieving 2% inflation has been subordinated to stimulating aggregate demand to promote economic recovery and prevent slippage into the second 'dip' of a 'double dip' recession.
- Monetary policy was generally successful prior to 2008, but has been largely unsuccessful since then.
- This recent lack of success may mean that the framework of monetary policy needs radical change, particularly in terms of the 2% inflation rate target.

Fiscal policy and supply-side policy

These notes, which relate to AQA specification section 3.4.2, prepare you to answer AQA examination questions on:

- the macroeconomic and microeconomic effects of fiscal policy
- interrelationships between fiscal policy and monetary policy

AQA A2 Economics

- the structure of taxation and public spending in the UK
- supply-side policy including supply-side fiscal policy

Essential information

What you already know about fiscal policy, taxation and public expenditure

When studying AS Unit 2 you learnt that fiscal policy attempts to achieve the policy objectives set by the government using the **fiscal instruments** of **government spending**, **taxation** and the government's **budgetary position** (balanced budget, budget deficit or budget surplus). You also learnt that fiscal policy can be used as a demand-side policy and that supply-side fiscal policy forms perhaps the most important part of a range of supply-side policies.

Demand-side fiscal policy

During the Keynesian era, fiscal policy was used primarily to manage the level of aggregate demand in the economy. When expanding or contracting aggregate demand, fiscal policy brings about a **multiplier effect**.

The government spending multiplier

Figure 10 illustrates how an increase in government spending (or in any component of aggregate demand) causes multiple successive changes in national income, greater in total than the initial increase in government spending. This is the multiplier.

To explain the multiplier, let us assume that there is demand-deficient unemployment, that the levels of taxation and imports are fixed, and that the government is initially balancing its budget (that is, $G = T$). To eliminate demand-deficient unemployment, the Keynesian government decides to run a budget deficit by spending an extra £10 billion on road building while keeping taxation unchanged.

- In the first stage of the multiplier process, income of £10 billion is received by building workers who, like everybody else in the economy, spend 90p of every pound of income on consumption. It is therefore assumed that the **marginal propensity to consume (MPC)** is 0.9 throughout the economy.
- At the second stage of the multiplier process, £9 billion of the £10 billion income is spent on consumer goods and services, with the remaining £1 billion leaking into unspent savings.
- At the third stage, consumer goods sector employees spend £8.1 billion, or 0.9 of the £9 billion received at the second stage of income generation.

Further stages of income generation then occur, with each successive stage being 0.9 of the previous stage. Each stage is smaller than the preceding stage to the extent that part of income leaks into savings. Assuming that nothing else changes in the time taken for the process to work through the economy, the eventual increase in income (ΔY) resulting from the initial injection of government spending (ΔG) is the sum of all the stages of income generation. ΔY is larger than, or a multiple of, ΔG, which triggered the initial growth in national income.

Knowledge check 21

What is demand-side policy?

Multiplier A multiplier exists whenever a change in one variable triggers multiple and successive changes in a second variable. The only multipliers you need to know are the national income multipliers.

Examiner tip

Neither the Unit 4 specification nor the Unit 2 specification requires students to possess knowledge of the marginal propensity to consume. Nevertheless, it is useful to possess this knowledge, and knowledge of related concepts such as the marginal propensity to save and the marginal propensity to import.

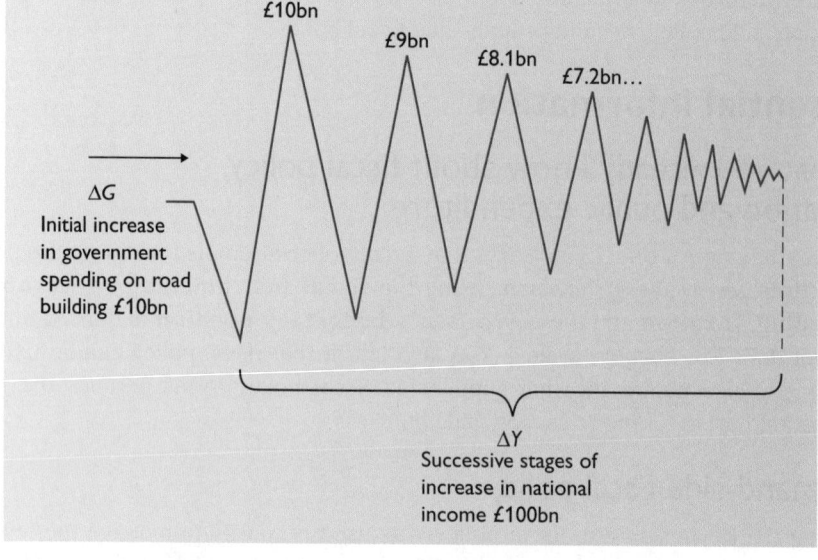

Figure 10 The government spending multiplier

The various national income multipliers

The **national income multiplier** is a general term covering a number of specific multipliers, each relating to a particular component of aggregate demand (or to a leakage of demand from the circular flow of income). The multipliers associated with changes in aggregate demand are the **consumption multiplier**, the **investment multiplier**, the **government spending multiplier** and the **export multiplier**. The multipliers associated with changes in leakages of demand are the **tax multiplier** and the **import multiplier**. These multipliers are negative. This means that an increase in taxation or imports leads to a multiple *fall* in national income. Taken together the government spending and tax multipliers are **fiscal policy multipliers**; the export and import multipliers are **foreign trade multipliers**.

The size of the multiplier and demand-side fiscal policy

Fiscal policy is most powerful for managing aggregate demand when the multiplier is large (for example, in Figure 10 the size of the multiplier is 10). In this situation, expansionary fiscal policy produces an increase in national income much larger than the increase in government spending or tax cut. However, in real life, demand-side fiscal policy is much less powerful, partly because fiscal multipliers are quite small — much closer to 1 than to 10.

Why the government spending multiplier is small

The government spending multiplier is small because, at each stage of the multiplier process, a large fraction of income leaks into imports and taxation as well as into savings, and is therefore not spent on consumption. Even more significantly, the multiplier process increases *nominal* national income, but not necessarily *real* national income. Depending on the slope of the *SRAS* curve and the nearness to full employment, the multiplier effect resulting from an increase in government spending may increase prices (in a demand-pull inflation) rather than output and jobs.

The decline of demand-side or Keynesian fiscal policy

In the 1970s, with the free-market revival and the influence of monetarist theories, UK governments stopped using fiscal policy to manage aggregate demand. They abandoned demand-side fiscal policy, partly because of the small size of the government spending multiplier, partly because they believed that increased government spending crowds out private sector spending, and partly because at the time increasing the budget deficit simply injected larger and larger doses of inflation into the economy, irrespective of boom or recession. (See also the coverage of the crisis in Keynesian economics on page 12.)

Keynesian fiscal policy: revival and further decline

Likewise, if you refer back to page 14, you will come across mention of **fiscal stimulus** and **fiscal austerity**. Fiscal stimulus refers to Keynesian fiscal policy unexpectedly coming into fashion once again as a means of 'spending the economy out of recession' following the massive collapse of aggregate demand in 2008 and 2009. The best that can be claimed for the fiscal stimulus is that it prevented the 2008 recession deepening into a full-blown depression. However, as page 14 mentions, the fiscal stimulus quickly led to a completely new problem, the **sovereign debt problem**. In 2010, the incoming Coalition government, dominated by the Conservatives, abandoned the fiscal stimulus, replacing it with the opposite policy of fiscal austerity. This involved, and continues to involve, swingeing public spending cuts and some tax increases. These were aimed at cutting the UK's budget deficit and the National Debt, in order to restore international confidence in the UK's ability to repay overseas-held debt.

Budget deficits, government borrowing and budget surpluses

Budget deficits have to be financed by borrowing. To a certain extent, the government borrows from the UK banking system. When banks lend to the government, they create new bank deposits for the government to spend. Bank deposits are money, so this increases the money supply.

Alternatively, the government borrows by selling government bonds (gilts) to pension funds and insurance companies. To finance a growing budget deficit, the government may have to raise interest rates offered on gilts. But this raises interest rates in general, which discourages private sector investment in capital goods. This is part of the crowding out process referred to earlier. To a large extent these days, UK governments borrow on overseas financial markets, leading to the sovereign debt problem referred to earlier.

Do not confuse *financing* a budget deficit with using higher taxes or reduced public spending to *eliminate* a budget deficit. Note also that when tax revenue exceeds public sector spending, a budget surplus results. Budget surpluses allow the government to repay past borrowings and to reduce the size of the National Debt.

Supply-side economic policy

Supply-side economic policy comprises the set of government policies which aim to improve the economic performance of the markets and industries that make up the economy, and also the performance and efficiency of individual firms and workers

Crowding out This is said to occur when an increase in public sector spending displaces and leads to a fall in private sector spending.

Examiner tip
While you are not expected to be familiar with the term 'sovereign debt', you are expected to be aware of events in the UK economy in the 10 years before the exam. Sovereign debt also affects the UK's relations with the EU and its global position.

Knowledge check 23
How are budget deficits and surpluses affected by the economic cycle?

Examiner tip
Because the UK has not enjoyed a budget surplus since the late 1990s, exam questions are more likely to focus on budget deficits and borrowing. The term 'National Debt' is not in the specification, but it is useful to know.

Examiner tip
Recent ECON 4 (and ECON 2) exams have often focused on supply-side policies, so it is important that you understand what they are. Be aware also that firms in the private sector, as well as the government, can also bring about supply-side reform.

within markets. Supply-side policies are favoured by free-market economists and politicians who reject interventionist Keynesian policies. Extreme supply-side economists completely reject Keynesian demand-side policies. While rejecting Keynesian demand management policies and intervention in the economy by 'big government', more moderate supply-side economists agree that monetary policy can still be used to manage aggregate demand. For the most part, supply-side policies are also microeconomic rather than simply macroeconomic, since, by acting on the motivation and efficiency of individual economic agents within the economy, the policies aim to change the underlying structure and competitiveness of the economy. Examples of microeconomic supply-side policies are deregulation and privatisation.

Supply-side economists, along with other supporters of the free-market revival, believe that a competitive economy is usually close to its equilibrium or natural levels of output and employment. However, due to distortions and inefficiencies resulting from Keynesian neglect of the supply side, towards the end of the Keynesian era these natural levels became unnecessarily low. To increase the natural levels of output and employment (and to reduce the natural rate of unemployment), supply-side economic policies must be used.

Supply-side fiscal policy

In the 1980s and until the temporary revival of Keynesian fiscal policy in the 2008 recession, supply-side fiscal policy replaced demand-side fiscal policy. Along with other examples of supply-side policy, supply-side fiscal policy tries to alter at the microeconomic level the incentives facing economic agents. Income tax cuts may make people work harder, while cuts in the real value of unemployment benefits (compared to disposable income in work) may encourage unskilled and low-paid workers to choose work rather than unemployment. Supply-side tax cuts may also encourage saving, investment and an entrepreneurial culture.

The Laffer curve

Laffer curve The curve is named after a famous supply-side economist, Professor Arthur Laffer.

Supply-side economists believe that high rates of income tax and the overall burden upon taxpayers create disincentives which, by reducing national income as taxation increases, also reduce the government's total tax revenue. This effect is illustrated by the Laffer curve in Figure 11.

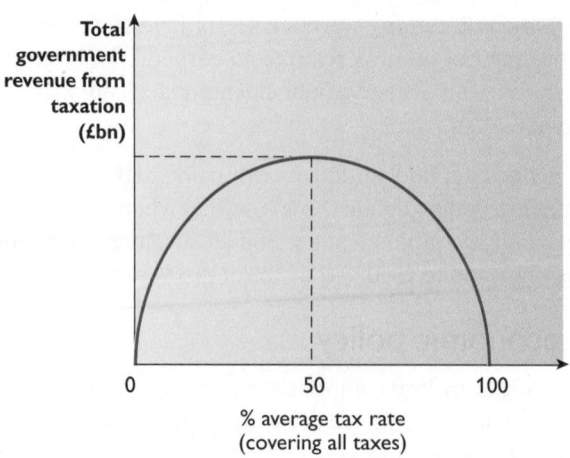

Figure 11 The Laffer curve

AQA A2 Economics

The Laffer curve shows how the government's total tax revenue changes as the average tax rate increases from 0% to 100%. Tax revenue must, of course, be zero when the average tax rate is 0%, but the diagram also shows that total tax revenue is again zero when the tax rate is 100%. With the average tax rate set at 100%, all income must be paid as tax to the government. In this situation, there is no incentive to produce output other than for subsistence, so with no output produced, the government ends up collecting no tax revenue.

Between the limiting tax rates of 0% and 100%, the Laffer curve shows tax revenue first rising and then falling as the average rate of taxation increases. Tax revenue is maximised at the highest point on the Laffer curve, which in Figure 11 occurs at an average tax rate (for all taxes) of 50%. Beyond this point, any further increase in the average tax rate becomes counterproductive, causing total tax revenue to fall. Tax rate cuts, by contrast, increase total tax revenue.

The Office for Budget Responsibility

Since May 1997, UK monetary policy has been implemented by an operationally independent Bank of England and its Monetary Policy Committee. The initial success of the MPC in controlling inflation led to the call by many economists and politicians for fiscal policy to be handed over to an independent Fiscal Commission. The Labour government in power at the time rejected this idea, setting up instead two **fiscal rules** by which the Treasury should abide.

The deterioration in government finances at the time of the 2008 recession meant that the two fiscal rules could not be met. The government therefore suspended the rules, hoping perhaps to bring them back in the future. Fiscal policy focused on the fiscal stimulus for the rest of the recession.

Instead of reviving the Labour government's fiscal rules, the Coalition government elected in 2010 replaced the rules with a newly created **Office for Budget Responsibility (OBR)**. The office was formed to make an independent assessment of the economy and the long-term sustainability of the public finances. The office published its first **annual Fiscal Sustainability Report (FSR)** in July 2011. The FSRs are meant to help inform the public on the long-term challenges facing the UK's public finances, though critics claim that neither the office nor its reports are free from pro-government bias.

Automatic stabilisers

These notes might seem to imply that governments must choose between demand-side and supply-side fiscal policy. This is not completely true. The reason for this lies in the role of **automatic stabilisers**, a role accepted by all recent UK governments. Suppose the economy enters recession. As national income falls and unemployment rises, **demand-led public spending** on unemployment and welfare benefits also rises. However, if the income tax system is progressive (see next page), the government's tax revenues fall faster than national income. In this way, increased public spending on transfers and declining tax revenues inject demand back into the economy, thereby stabilising and dampening the deflationary impact of the initial fall in aggregate demand, and reducing the overall size of the contractionary multiplier effect.

Automatic stabilisers also operate in the opposite direction to dampen the expansionary effects of an increase in aggregate demand. As incomes and employment

increase, the take-up of 'means-tested' welfare benefits and unemployment pay falls automatically, while at the same time tax revenues rise faster than income. Demand is taken out of the economy and the size of the expansionary multiplier is reduced.

Direct and indirect taxation

Income tax is a direct tax because the person who receives and benefits from the income is liable to pay the tax. By contrast, most **expenditure taxes** are indirect taxes since the seller of the good, and not the purchaser who benefits from its consumption, is liable to pay the tax. Nevertheless, the purchaser *indirectly* pays some or all of the tax when the seller passes on the incidence of the tax through a price rise.

Progressive, regressive and proportionate taxation

In a **progressive tax system**, the proportion of a person's income paid in tax increases as income rises, while in a **regressive tax system**, the proportion paid in tax falls. A tax is proportionate if exactly the same proportion of income is paid in tax at all levels of income. Progressiveness can be defined for a single tax or for the tax system as a whole. For income tax to be progressive, the *marginal rate* at which the tax is levied must be higher than the *average rate* — though the average rate, which measures the proportion of income paid in tax, rises as income increases. Conversely, with a regressive income tax, the marginal rate of tax is less than the average rate, while the two are equal in the case of a proportionate tax. As a general rule, the average tax rate indicates the overall burden of the tax on the taxpayer, but the marginal rate may affect economic choice and decision making significantly, influencing incentives and the choice between work and leisure and decisions about how much labour to supply.

Progressive taxation and the distribution of income

Progressive taxation cannot by itself redistribute income — a policy of **transfers** in the government's public expenditure programme is required for this. Progressive taxation used on its own merely reduces post-tax income differentials compared to pre-tax differentials. It is often assumed that the UK tax system is highly progressive, being used by governments to reduce inequalities in income and wealth. In fact, wealth taxation (or capital taxation) is almost non-existent in the UK, so inequalities in the distribution of wealth have hardly been affected by the tax system. Many people believe that direct taxes are strongly progressive in the UK, but this is untrue. Direct taxes, which for the most part are income taxes, are only slightly progressive for most income groups, becoming mildly regressive for the richest fifth of households. In 2010 the introduction of a 50% marginal tax rate on taxable income above £150,000 — a response to the deterioration in government finances — marginally increased the progressivity of UK income tax, though supply-side economists are calling for abolition of the 50% tax rate. Because indirect taxes are mostly regressive, taking a declining proportion of the income of rich households, overall the UK tax system may even be slightly regressive.

Examination questions and skills

Along with monetary policy, fiscal policy and supply-side policy are important parts of the Unit 4 specification. Some examination questions obviously focus on fiscal policy and supply-side policy as policy *instruments*. Questions on policy *objectives*, such as growth, full employment and price stability, also require knowledge and understanding of fiscal and supply-side policies as means to achieve these objectives.

Common examination errors

- Assuming that fiscal policy always means demand management.
- A lack of awareness of the supply-side elements of modern fiscal policy.
- Failing to understand interrelationships between fiscal policy and monetary policy.
- A lack of a wider understanding of supply-side policies other than supply-side fiscal policy.
- Defining progressive taxation incorrectly.
- Failing to appreciate the synoptic linkages between fiscal policy in Unit 4 and Unit 3 topics such as market failures and income distribution.

- Fiscal policy is the use of the fiscal instruments of government spending and taxation to achieve economic policy objectives.
- Fiscal policy can be divided into demand-side and supply-side fiscal policy.
- Demand-side fiscal policy, often called Keynesian fiscal policy, aims to manage aggregate demand.
- The government spending multiplier is a key concept for analysing demand-side fiscal policy.
- Demand-side fiscal policy went out of fashion in the 1980s but was temporarily revived in the 2008 recession.

- Free-market economists reject demand-side fiscal policy, preferring instead supply-side fiscal policy.
- The Laffer curve and its implications for tax policy are key elements of supply-side fiscal policy.
- Supply-side fiscal policy is just one element of supply-side policies.
- Most economists accept the automatic stabilising role of fiscal policy.
- Taxes can be direct or indirect, progressive, regressive or proportionate.

Summary

International trade, globalisation and the EU

These notes, which relate to AQA specification section 3.4.3, prepare you to answer AQA examination questions on:
- comparative advantage, and the case for and against international trade
- the pattern of international trade
- the impact of globalisation on the UK and world economies
- the European Union as a customs union and the Single European Market (SEM)

Essential information

What you already know about international trade

When studying AS Unit 1: Markets and Market Failure, you learnt that specialisation and the division of labour can increase production possibilities and economic welfare. In Unit 2: The National Economy, you learnt that an increase in exports shifts the

aggregate demand curve to the right, but that an increase in imports has the opposite effect, taking demand out of the domestic economy.

Closed economies

A country that does not take part in international trade is called a **closed economy**. The goods and services which its inhabitants can consume are limited to those which its resource base allows it to produce. If the country is small, average costs of production are likely to be high because small population size and the absence of export markets mean that **economies of scale** and **long production runs** cannot be achieved.

Open economies

A country which trades freely with other countries is called an **open economy**. Imports of raw materials and energy widen an open economy's production possibilities greatly, though in practice, open economies concentrate on producing the goods and services that they are good at producing, and import other goods and services. By exporting the goods they can produce competitively, open economies benefit from economies of scale and long production runs gained from access to the much larger world market. Likewise, imports lead to a vast array of choice and the possibility of a much higher level of economic welfare and living standards than is possible in a world without trade.

Widening choice

International trade between open economies thus increases each country's **production possibilities**, and also its consumption possibilities. According to its advocates, free trade widens choice for both producers and consumers, and facilitates faster rates of economic growth. To explain these benefits further, two important economic principles must be introduced: the **division of labour**, and **absolute and comparative advantage**.

Specialisation and the division of labour

When a worker specialises, he or she is employed to perform a narrow range of tasks: for example, teaching economics. Specialisation leads to a division of labour, in which different workers do different types of work. It also involves regional specialisation *within* a country: for example, the City of London specialises in producing financial services. Finally, there is international specialisation *between* countries, in which different countries specialise in different industries and then trade their surpluses. The international division of labour and successful specialisation reduce costs of production, and contribute to the widening of production and consumption possibilities.

Absolute advantage

If a country is best at (or technically and productively efficient at) producing a good or service, it possesses an absolute advantage in the good's production. Absolute advantage must not be confused with the rather more subtle concept of comparative advantage.

Consumption possibilities These depict the different goods and services available for people to purchase. Assuming limited income, the opportunity cost of purchasing one good is measured by the other goods sacrificed or forgone.

Examiner tip
Be prepared to apply synoptically the microeconomic concepts of production possibilities, economies and diseconomies of scale, and increasing and decreasing returns to scale.

Comparative advantage

To explain comparative advantage, let us pretend that the world economy comprises just two countries, Oceana and Eurasia, each with just two units of resource (for example, man-years of labour), which can produce only two commodities, guns and butter. Each unit of resource, or indeed a fraction of each unit (because it is assumed that resources or inputs are divisible), can be switched from one industry to another if so desired in each country. Finally, the production possibilities of 1 unit of resource are:

| In Oceana: | 6 guns | or | 2 tons of butter |
| In Eurasia: . | 1 gun | or | 4 tons of butter |

In terms of technical efficiency, Oceana is 'best at' – or has an absolute advantage in – gun production, while Eurasia's absolute advantage lies in butter production. In this particular example, Oceana also has a comparative advantage in guns and Eurasia has a comparative advantage in butter. Comparative advantage is measured in terms of **opportunity cost**, or what a country gives up when it increases the output of an industry by 1 unit.

Ask yourself how many guns Oceana would have to stop producing or give up in order to increase its butter output by 1 ton. The answer is 3 guns, but Eurasia would only have to give up a quarter of a gun to produce an extra ton of butter. Similarly, the opportunity cost of one extra gun in Eurasia is 4 tons of butter sacrificed, but the opportunity cost of an extra gun in Oceana is only a third of a ton of butter. This tells us that Oceana has a comparative advantage in gun production and Eurasia has a comparative advantage in butter production.

Output gains from specialisation

Without specialisation, Oceana and Eurasia together produce 7 guns and 6 tons of butter (assuming each country devotes 1 unit of resource to each industry). If each country specialises in the industry in which it has a comparative advantage, total output changes to 12 guns and 8 tons of butter: that is, a *gain* of 5 guns and 2 tons of butter. (Even if it had been assumed that Oceana possessed an absolute advantage in producing *both* guns and butter, specialisation could still lead to an output gain, but only if opportunity costs differ in the two countries, so that comparative advantage can be identified.)

Import controls or protectionism

Import controls can be divided into **quantity controls** such as **import quotas**, which put a maximum limit on imports, and **tariffs** (**import duties**) and their opposite **export subsidies**, which respectively raise the price of imports or reduce the price of exports.

The case against import controls

Supporters of free trade believe that import controls prevent countries from specialising in activities in which they have a comparative advantage and then trading their surpluses. As a result, production takes place inefficiently, and the growth of economic welfare is reduced.

Comparative advantage The country that gives up *least* of other goods when increasing output of a particular good possesses the comparative advantage in that good.

Knowledge check 24

What is meant by opportunity cost?

Examiner tip

While exam questions are frequently set on the case for free trade, think carefully before you introduce into your answer a numerical example of comparative advantage. Students often spend too much time on this, and in any case the examples are often riddled with mistakes. A clear statement of the meaning of comparative advantage may be all the question requires.

Knowledge check 25

What is meant by economic welfare?

Examiner tip

The case for import controls is, of course, the same as the case against free trade. Likewise, the case for free trade is the same as the case against import controls. Expect exam questions on either issue.

Competitive advantage Refers to countries producing goods which are quality competitive, often embodying good design and the latest technology. Consumers want to buy the goods, even if they are sometimes sold at higher prices than rival products. Mercedes cars and iphones are examples.

Knowledge check 26

Distinguish between increasing and decreasing returns to scale.

The case for import controls

Increasing returns to scale and the 'infant industry' argument

The case for free trade depends to a large extent on some of the assumptions underlying the principle of comparative advantage. Destroy these assumptions and the case for free trade is weakened. One assumption is **constant returns to scale**. In the numerical example above, 1 unit of resource produces 6 guns or 2 tons of butter in Oceana, whether it is the first unit of resource employed or the millionth unit.

However, in the real world, it is arguable that **increasing returns to scale** are more common than constant returns to scale. In a world of increasing returns to scale, the more a country specialises in a particular industry, the more efficient it becomes in that industry, thereby increasing its comparative advantage. At first sight, this increases the case for international specialisation and trade. However, increasing returns to scale can also justify import controls for developing countries attempting to promote the growth of new industries.

This is the **infant industry** argument. According to this argument, new industries, which in poor countries have not as yet developed increasing returns to scale, need protecting from giant firms in developed countries, where increasing returns to scale have significantly reduced average costs of production. In the 1980s, the infant industry argument developed into a more sophisticated **strategic trade theory**, which argues that a country's competitive advantage (and thence its *comparative* advantage) is often not 'natural' or 'God-given'. Rather, governments create competitive advantage by nurturing strategically selected industries or economic sectors, typically those that make high-tech goods and use skilled labour. However, the selected sectors must be protected from international competition while they are built up. The skills and expertise thus gained then spill over to help other sectors in the economy.

Decreasing returns to scale

When **decreasing returns to scale** occur, specialisation erodes efficiency and destroys any initial comparative advantage. A good example occurs in agriculture when over-specialisation results in monoculture, in which the growing of a single cash crop for export may lead to soil erosion, vulnerability to pests and falling agricultural yields in the future.

Over-specialisation may also cause a country to become particularly vulnerable to sudden changes in demand or to changes in the cost and availability of imported raw materials or energy. Changes in costs, and new inventions and technical progress, can eliminate a country's comparative advantage. The principle of comparative advantage implicitly assumes relatively stable demand and cost conditions. The greater the uncertainty about the future, the weaker is the case for complete specialisation.

The self-sufficiency argument

If a country is self-sufficient in all important respects, it is effectively neutralised against the danger of importing recession and unemployment from the rest of the world if international demand collapses. Protection may also be necessary for military and strategic reasons to ensure that a country is relatively self-sufficient in vital foodstuffs, energy and raw materials in time of war.

Protecting declining industries

An argument opposite to the infant industry argument is sometimes made in advanced industrial economies to protect **sunset industries** in the older industrial regions from competition from new industries in developing countries. Keynesian economists have sometimes advocated the selective use of import controls as a potentially effective supply-side policy instrument to prevent unnecessary **deindustrialisation** and to allow orderly rather than disruptive structural change in the manufacturing base of the economy. They have also argued that it is better to employ labour inefficiently than for it to remain unemployed.

The anti-dumping argument

Some economists also justify import controls to protect an economy from **dumping**: that is, goods being sold below cost to get rid of excess supply in the exporting country.

Protecting an economy from importing demerit goods and 'bads'

In addition, as demerit goods (e.g. narcotic drugs) and 'bads' (e.g. industrial waste) clearly indicate, an *output* gain does not necessarily lead to a *welfare* gain. Governments believe that they have a moral duty to ban imports of heroin, cocaine and handguns, to protect the welfare of their citizens.

The pattern of world trade

The 'North/South' pattern of world trade

To many people living in industrial countries during the nineteenth century and the first half of the twentieth century, it must have seemed almost 'natural' that the earliest countries to industrialise, such as Britain, had done so because they possessed a comparative advantage in manufacturing. It probably seemed equally 'natural' that a pattern of world trade should have developed in which industrialised countries in what is now called the **North** exported manufactured goods in exchange for foodstuffs and raw materials produced by countries whose comparative advantage lay in the production of primary products — the countries of the **South**, or developing countries.

The 'North/North' pattern of world trade

The actual pattern of world trade changed in the latter part of the twentieth century and the early years of the twenty-first century from **North/South exchange** of manufactured goods for primary products. Most of the trade of the developed industrial economies is now between themselves and newly industrialised countries (NICs); only a relatively small amount is with the rest of the world. Much world trade is now **North/North** — high-income developed economies trading mostly with each other — though another important feature of modern world trade results from the shift of manufacturing industries to China and to other Asian economies. Some

Examiner tip
Another way of answering an exam question on patterns of trade is to focus on the pattern of trade in different goods and services, such as oil. Also, don't confuse the UK's pattern of trade with global trade patterns.

commentators have recently drawn attention to the recent growth of **South/South** trade, in which African countries and Brazil trade increasingly with each other.

Globalisation

Globalisation is the process integrating all or most of the world's economies and making countries increasingly dependent on each other. Globalisation's main features are:

- the growth of international trade and the reduction of trade barriers — a process encouraged by the World Trade Organization (WTO)
- greater international mobility of capital
- a significant increase in the power of international capitalism and multinational corporations (MNCs)
- a decrease in governmental power over MNCs

Free-market economists generally support globalisation, regarding it as inevitable and the major process through which economic development can occur in poor countries. Opponents argue that globalisation is a respectable name for the growing exploitation of the world's poor by international capitalism and American economic and cultural imperialism — though China is fast taking over America's mantle in this respect.

Critics of globalisation use the **dependency theory of trade and development** to argue that developing countries possess little capital because the system of world trade and payments has been organised by developed industrial economies to their own advantage. Until recently, export and import prices generally moved in favour of industrialised countries and against primary producers. This means that by exporting the same amount of goods and services to the South, a developed economy can import a greater quantity of raw materials or foodstuffs in exchange. From a developing country's point of view, it must export more in order to buy the same quantity of capital goods or energy, vital for development.

(For further information about globalisation, see the answer to Essay Question 7 in the Questions and Answers section of this guide.)

The European Union as a customs union

Free trade areas and customs unions

The **European Union (EU)** started life in the 1950s as a **customs union**. At the time, the UK was not a member of the EU (which was then known as the European Economic Community (EEC)), preferring instead to belong to a **free trade area**, which is another type of trading bloc. In a free trade area, member countries abolish tariffs on mutual trade, but each partner determines its own import controls on trade with non-member countries. A customs union also creates intra-union free trade, but takes away members' freedom to set their own tariffs against non-member states. Instead, all members of the customs union impose a **common external tariff** on trade with non-members. Free trade areas and customs unions are examples of **trading blocs**.

The Single European Market

In 1993, with the creation of the **Single European Market (SEM)**, the EU developed into a fuller common market. It did this by creating free internal trade in services as

AQA A2 Economics

well as in goods, together with largely free mobility of capital and labour between EU member states. The **European Commission (EC)** is responsible for the smooth operation of the SEM. The EC is the EU's executive body, akin to the UK civil service, and implements EU economic policy to meet the requirements of EU political institutions such as the Council of Ministers. Currently, there are 27 Commissioners, each appointed by a different EU country and each with a specific responsibility such as agriculture or trade.

Examination questions and skills

Because the Unit title is 'The National and International Economy', at least one of the three essay questions in each examination is likely to be on international economics. Additionally, as their names indicate, the Global Context and EU Context data-response questions inevitably have international dimensions, though these questions focus on the impact of one or more international issues on the UK macro economy. The five main topics to revise in the context of international trade are: the benefits and costs of international trade (particularly in relation to comparative advantage); the case for and against import controls; how the pattern of international trade has changed; the impact of globalisation on the UK and world economies; and the impact of the UK's membership of the EU on the UK's trade (and its wider economic performance).

Common examination errors

- Writing descriptive accounts of the benefits of free trade devoid of theoretical underpinning analysis.
- Confusing comparative advantage with absolute advantage.
- Failing to appreciate the limitations of the principle of comparative advantage.
- Writing overlong and numerically inaccurate illustrations of comparative advantage.
- Assuming that free trade is advantageous for all countries, at all times.
- Assuming that countries should always try to maximise exports and minimise imports.
- Asserting without sufficient evidence that globalisation is always good or bad.
- Wrongly describing the European Union as a free trade area rather than as a customs union.

Examiner tip

Likely EU topics to feature in the ECON 4 exam are the euro and the eurozone. The final topic in this Guide covers these. However, at the time of writing, pressures on the euro have grown to such an extent that by the time you read this Guide, the eurozone may no longer exist.

Summary

- Most economists believe that international free trade benefits all countries and increases the economic welfare of their inhabitants.
- Some economists dispute this and argue that there is sometimes a case for import controls.
- The principle of comparative advantage provides the main theoretical argument for free trade.
- Increasing and decreasing returns to scale provide a justification for import controls.

- In recent decades, the North/South pattern of world trade has to a large extent been replaced by North/North trade.
- Free trade, encouraged by the World Trade Organization, is perhaps the most important contributor to the process of globalisation.
- The European Union started life as a customs union with internal free trade but protected by a common external tariff.

The balance of payments, exchange rates and the euro

These notes, which relate to AQA specification section 3.4.3, prepare you to answer AQA examination questions on:

- the difference between the current account and capital flows in the balance of payments
- how the exchange rate is determined in floating and fixed exchange rate systems
- the European Union's single currency and economic and monetary union (EMU)

Essential information

What you already know about the balance of payments, exchange rates and EMU

When studying AS Unit 2 you learnt briefly about the current account of the balance of payments, and about how changes in interest rates (in monetary policy) and the exchange rate can affect the current account. However, Unit 2 did not cover capital flows; nor did it cover EMU and the euro.

The current and capital accounts of the balance of payments

The balance of payments measures all the currency flows into and out of an economy within a particular time period, usually a year. Until quite recently, the UK government divided the balance of payments into two main categories:

- the **current account**
- the **capital account**

To fit in with the IMF method of classification, capital flows, which comprised the old capital account, now form the **financial account** of the balance of payments, and the term 'capital account' is now used to categorise various transfers of income that were previously part of the current account before the new method of classification was adopted. Table 1 shows the current method of classification for 2009.

The current account

The current account measures the flow of expenditure on goods and services, thus showing the country's income gained and lost from trade. The current account is usually regarded as the most important part of the balance of payments because it reflects the economy's international competitiveness and the extent to which a country is living within its means. Ignoring the other items in the current account, if receipts from exports are less than payments for imports, there is a **current account deficit**, whereas if receipts exceed payments, there is a **current account surplus**.

The balance of trade

The main items in the current account are the **balance of trade in goods** and the **balance of trade in services**. The current account balance is largely determined

---

Capital flows

Movements of currency out of a country to invest in overseas assets such as factories and shopping malls, the takeover of overseas companies, and bonds issued by foreign government.

Examiner tip

Exam questions are likely to focus on the current account of the balance of payments rather than on capital flows.

by adding these together. **Trade in goods** is sometimes called **visible trade**, and trade in services is called **invisible trade**. As Table 1 shows, the UK has a visible trade deficit and an invisible trade surplus. Particularly before the financial crisis that accompanied and partially caused recession in 2008, the earnings of financial services in the City of London contributed significantly to the invisible trade surplus. In most years, the invisible surplus is insufficient to offset the visible deficit, so the current account taken as a whole is also in deficit.

Table 1 Selected items from the UK balance of payments, 2010 (£m)

The current account (*mostly trade flows*)	
Balance of trade in goods	−98,462
Balance of trade in services	+58,778
Net income flows	+23,428
Net current transfers	−20,081
Balance of payments on the current account	**−36,726**
The capital account	
(transfers, which used to be in the current account)	**+3,708**
The financial account (capital flows, which used to be in the capital account)	
Net direct investment	+21,804
Net portfolio investment	+10,434
Other capital flows (including short-term 'hot money' flows)	−15,349
Drawings on reserves	−6,070
Financial account balance	**+41,517**
The balance (errors and omissions)	**+8,949**

Source: Balance of Payments, *2011 Pink Book*, November 2011

Net income flows

Net **income flows** provide an important link between the current account and capital flows. British residents (including UK-based multinational companies) invest in capital assets located in other countries. Investment in capital assets is a **capital flow** (see below), but income generated by overseas capital assets is part of the current account. Net income flows are the difference between these inward income flows to UK residents from capital assets owned overseas and outward profit flows to companies such as Toyota, generated by the assets they own in the UK.

Capital flows

Long-term direct capital flows occur when residents of one country invest in productive resources such as factories located abroad. Such investment can be either **direct investment** or **portfolio investment**.

Direct investment

A direct *outward* capital flow occurs when UK firms invest in productive capacity in other countries — this is known as outward direct investment. Conversely, the

purchase by foreign firms of new factories etc. in the UK is an example of *inward direct capital investment* — this is usually known as foreign direct investment.

Portfolio investment

In contrast to direct investment, **portfolio investment** involves the purchase of financial assets rather than physical assets.

Short-term investment or 'hot money' capital flows

Direct investment and portfolio investment are treated as **long-term capital flows**. Table 1 shows that in 2010, when inward and outward direct and portfolio capital flows were added up, more long-term investment flowed into the UK than flowed out. Long-term capital flows are largely a response to comparative advantage, reflecting people's decisions to invest in economic activities and industries located in countries to which comparative advantage has moved. However, since changes in comparative advantage usually take place quite slowly, long-term capital flows tend to be relatively stable and predictable.

The same is not true of **short-term capital flows**, which are largely speculative. These flows occur because the owners of funds believe that, by taking advantage of interest rate differences and by gambling on future changes in exchange rates, they can make a quick speculative profit or capital gain by moving funds out of one currency and into another. Partly because of their speculative nature and partly because a sudden change in market sentiment can turn an inflow into an outflow, short-term capital flows are also called **'hot money' flows**.

Balance of payments equilibrium

Balance of payments equilibrium refers to the current account and not to the *whole* of the balance of payments. The current account is in equilibrium when export earnings and inward income flows more or less equal payments for imports and outward income flows. **Disequilibrium** occurs when there is a large deficit or surplus on current account. A large current account deficit may, however, be quite stable — providing it is financed by inward capital flows. As Table 1 shows, the net capital inflow of £47,587 million more than financed the current account deficit of £36,726 million.

Balance of payments 'balance'

Do not confuse balance of payments equilibrium with balance of payments *balance*. Like any balance sheet, the balance of payments must exactly balance in the sense that all the items included in the balance sheet must sum to zero. The final item in Table 1 explains this. The number in the balance (errors and omissions) item is simply the number required to make all the items in the table sum to zero. Note also the relatively small size of the drawings on reserves item. This item shows that in 2009 the Bank of England sold pounds, using them to purchase reserves of foreign currencies. Central bank intervention in foreign exchange markets by selling or buying reserves is largely determined by whether the exchange rate is floating or fixed. Supporting a fixed exchange rate sometimes requires large-scale selling of reserves, but this is not the case with a freely floating exchange rate. Since 1992, the pound has floated freely; hence the relatively small size of changes in reserves.

Exchange rates

Exchange rates and a foreign exchange market exist because different countries use different currencies to pay for international trade. A currency's **exchange rate** is simply its external price, expressed in terms of another currency such as the US dollar, or gold, or indeed in terms of an artificial unit such as the **sterling index**, which is the weighted average of a sample of exchange rates of countries with which the UK trades.

Freely floating exchange rates

With **freely floating** (cleanly floating) exchange rates, the external value of a country's currency is determined on foreign exchange markets by the forces of demand and supply alone. Figure 12 illustrates how both the exchange rate and the current account of the balance of payments are determined in a freely floating system — subject to the very artificial assumption that there are no capital flows. If demand for pounds is D and supply is S_1, the equilibrium exchange rate, expressed against the US dollar, is $1.50. Assuming exports and imports are the only items in the current account of the balance of payments, the current account is also in equilibrium. The value of exports equalling the value of imports is £10 billion at the equilibrium exchange rate. When there are no capital flows, exchange rate equilibrium implies balance of payments equilibrium on the current account and vice versa.

Exchange rate The external price of a currency in terms of another currency or currencies.

Examiner tip
Because floating exchange rates are more common than fixed exchange rates, essay questions are generally set on floating exchange rates. However, Global and EU Context questions might mention how China, an emerging market country, has a semi-fixed exchange rate against the dollar, and how some non-eurozone countries (e.g. Poland) have semi-fixed exchange rates against the euro.

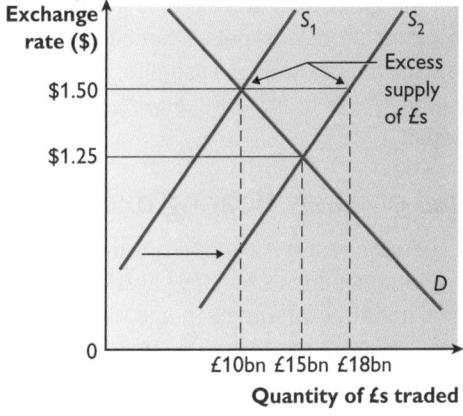

Figure 12 Exchange rate determination on a freely floating exchange rate system

How a freely floating exchange rate eliminates a current account deficit

Suppose that some event or shock disturbs this initial equilibrium — for example, an improvement in the quality of foreign-produced goods causing UK residents to increase their demand for imports at all existing sterling prices. Because the demand for foreign exchange to pay for imports increases, the supply curve of pounds shifts to the right from S_1 to S_2. At the exchange rate of $1.50, the current account is in deficit by £8 billion, which is also the excess supply of pounds on the foreign exchange market.

The market mechanism now swings into action to eliminate this excess supply, thereby restoring equilibrium, both for the exchange rate and for the current account.

The selling of pounds to get rid of excess supply causes the exchange rate to fall, which increases the price competitiveness of British exports and reduces that of imports. The adjustment process continues until a new equilibrium exchange rate is reached at $1.25 to the pound, with exports and imports both equalling £15 billion. Conversely, if the initial equilibrium were disturbed by an event that increased the demand for pounds and moved the current account into surplus, the exchange rate would rise to relieve the resulting excess demand for sterling, creating a new equilibrium at a higher exchange rate.

The advantages of freely floating exchange rates

- When the exchange rate is freely floating, current account surpluses and deficits cease to be a policy problem for governments and a constraint holding back the pursuit of the domestic economic objectives of full employment and growth. The government simply allows market forces to look after the balance of payments, while it concentrates on domestic economic policy. And if, in the pursuit of the domestic objectives of full employment and growth, the inflation rate rises out of line with other countries, the exchange rate falls to restore competitiveness.
- With a floating exchange rate, monetary policy can be completely independent of external conditions and influences. There is no need to keep official reserves to support the exchange rate or to finance a payments deficit. The country's domestic money supply is unaffected by a change in official reserves, and interest rate policy is not determined by the need to protect the exchange rate. The country is free to pursue an independent monetary policy aimed at achieving purely domestic economic objectives, without the need to assign monetary policy and interest rates to support the exchange rate or to attract capital flows into the country to finance a current account deficit.

The disadvantages of freely floating exchange rates

- The argument that a freely floating exchange rate can never be overvalued or undervalued for very long depends crucially on the assumption that speculation and capital flows have no influence on exchange rates. This assumption is wrong. Most foreign exchange deals relate to capital flows and not trade, and exchange rates have become extremely vulnerable to speculative capital or 'hot money' movements. A massive inward capital flow can overvalue an exchange rate and create a serious deficit on the current account.
- Floating exchange rates may unleash a vicious spiral of ever-faster inflation and exchange rate depreciation. Rising import prices caused by a falling exchange rate cause the domestic inflation rate to increase, which erodes the export competitiveness won by the initial depreciation of the exchange rate. A further fall in the exchange rate is then required to recover the lost advantage — and so on.

Fixed exchange rates

Figure 13 shows how a government and its central bank maintain a fixed exchange rate. Initially, the government fixes the exchange rate at a central peg of $2.00. Supply and demand determine the day-to-day exchange rate. Providing the exchange rate stays between a ceiling and a floor set when the fixed exchange rate was announced, there is no need for intervention by the central bank and the exchange rate is correctly

Examiner tip
Exam questions often ask for an evaluation of the advantages and disadvantages of floating exchange rates. Think of the advantages of floating exchange rates as the same as the disadvantages of fixed exchange rates, and the advantages of fixed exchange as the same as the disadvantages of floating exchange rates.

valued for trade. However, Figure 13 also shows the exchange rate falling to the floor of $1.98, possibly because of a speculative capital flow against the currency. At this point the central bank intervenes, raising domestic interest rates to attract capital flows into the currency, and using reserves to support the fixed exchange rate. By selling reserves and buying its own currency, the central bank creates an artificial demand for its own currency.

Persistent support for the currency means that the exchange rate is overvalued, condemning the country to overpriced exports, underpriced imports and a current account deficit. **Devaluation** is a policy solution — in this case, devaluation to a new central peg at $1.00. Alternatively, the government could abandon the fixed exchange rate and allow the currency to float downwards and find its own level. Although previously the pound's exchange is not fixed, in recent years the UK government seems to have encouraged the exchange rate to fall in an attempt to bring about export-led growth which might drag the economy out of recession.

Examiner tip
Don't confuse an exchange rate *system* such as a floating exchange rate system, with the definition of an exchange rate as the external price of a currency in terms of other currencies that it can buy.

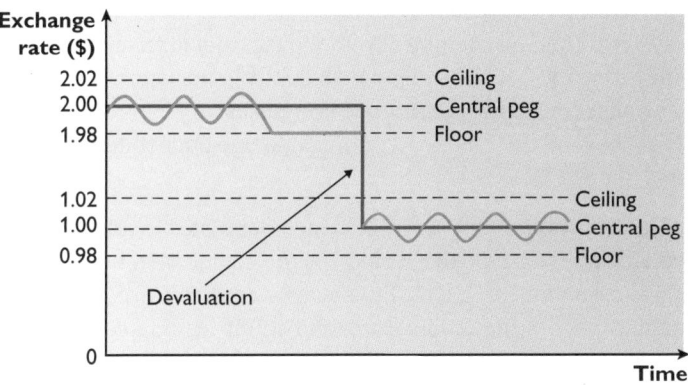

Figure 13 A fixed exchange rate

Economic and Monetary Union (EMU) and the euro

The crisis that hit the eurozone countries in 2011 makes it much more likely that the eurozone will break up than that the UK will adopt the euro.

The acronym EMU stands for **Economic and Monetary Union**, which means that monetary union is regarded by its supporters as a 'stepping stone' to a much fuller economic union within the EU. The single currency (the **euro**) lies at the heart of the monetary union. In 2011, EU countries divided into two groups. Most 'older' EU countries were in the **eurozone**, but the UK was among those choosing to remain outside the zone and to keep their national currencies. The eurozone countries are subject to a **common monetary policy** implemented by the **European Central Bank (ECB)** in Frankfurt.

Eurozone Also called the 'euro area', the eurozone comprises the EU member states such as Germany which use the euro rather than a national currency.

The 'one size fits all' problem

Eurozone member countries can no longer implement independent monetary policies. In an important sense, national central banks such as the Bundesbank (in Germany) and the Bank of France are now branch banks of the European Central Bank, which sets interest rates for the whole of the eurozone. This has led to the 'one

size fits all' problem. Without the convergence of economic cycles in the different eurozone countries, each country might be in a different phase of its economic cycle, with some countries in recession or on the verge of recession, while others are in the recovery or boom phases of the economic cycle. Without convergence, a high interest rate is needed to dampen demand-pull inflationary pressures in fast-growing countries, while low interest rates are required to stimulate economic recovery or to ward off recession in other countries. The 'one size fits all' problem stems from the fact that these requirements are mutually exclusive. In the outcome, the needs of core economies, particularly Germany and France, tend to override the requirements of periphery countries such as Ireland or Portugal.

The 'eurozone crisis'

For several years after its creation in 1998 and the first use of euro notes and coins in 2002, the euro and the eurozone appeared to be working well, facilitating the growth of free trade in Europe. However, a possibly fatal flaw lay hidden within the eurozone, which, when it emerged after the 2008/09 recession, threatened to destroy the system. The flaw stemmed from the fact that for a monetary union with a single currency to work, centralised political control and a common fiscal policy are required. Centralised political control became necessary to prevent countries such as Greece living beyond their means, running up huge budget deficits and borrowing far too much.

Also, a successful monetary union requires member states to adopt a common fiscal policy to redistribute some of the wealth of the richer members of the monetary union to its poorer members. Used in this way, a common fiscal policy maintains a degree of stability across the union. Eurozone countries possessed neither of these essential requirements for a successful monetary union. Consequently, by late 2011 the eurozone was on the verge of breaking down. By the time you sit your ECON 4 exam, the eurozone may no longer exist, at least in its original form.

Examination questions and skills

Examination questions are often set on the balance of payments and the exchange rate, and on the linkages between the two. A Global Context data-response question could test your knowledge and understanding of the causes (and/or the effects) of changes in the pound's exchange rate against the US dollar, or against a selection of world currencies. Similarly, an EU Context question could do the same with regard to the pound/euro exchange rate. The balance of payments and exchange rates are also likely to figure in one of the three essay questions.

Common examination errors

- Confusing the current account of the balance of payments with capital flows.
- Failing to appreciate the links between the current account and capital flows.
- Confusing current account equilibrium with balance on the balance of payments.
- Failing to understand how a floating exchange rate may eliminate a current account deficit.
- Writing one-sided polemical essays for or against EMU and the euro.

Examiner tip

Because of the 15-month time lag between setting and sitting exam papers, a question on the euro may well be out of date by the time you sit the paper. See the EU Context question in the June 2010 ECON 4 exam.

Summary

- The balance of payments, which divides into two main parts, the current account and capital flows, measures all the currency flows into and out of an economy in a particular time period, usually a year.

- The current account is usually regarded as the most important part of the balance of payments because it reflects the country's competitiveness.

- The most important parts of the current account are exports and imports. When $X < M$, the current account is usually in deficit, though other items in the current account such as income flows also have to be taken into account.

- Balance of payments equilibrium (roughly when $X = M$) must not be confused with balance of payments 'balance'.

- Capital flows divide into long-term direct and portfolio investment flows, together with short-term 'hot money' capital flows, which are often highly destabilising.

- The exchange rate, which is the external price of the currency against other currencies, can be either freely floating or fixed.

- In theory, and providing there are no capital flows (an unrealistic assumption), changes in a freely floating exchange rate automatically eliminate a current account deficit or surplus.

- The European Union (EU) began as a customs union (a form of trading bloc) before moving towards the fuller economic union of its member states.

- The creation of Economic and Monetary Union and the single currency, the euro, was seen as a stepping stone to fuller economic union.

- In 2011, the 'eurozone crisis' created uncertainty as to whether the eurozone and monetary union will survive.

Questions & Answers

The **ECON 4 exam**

The ECON 4 exam is 2 hours long and has a maximum mark of 80. The exam paper contains two sections, A and B, both of which must be answered. **Section A**, which accounts for 40 marks (50% of the total), comprises two **Context** data-response questions (DRQs), of which you must answer one. **Context 1** is **The Global Context** and **Context 2** is **The European Union Context**. **Section B**, which also accounts for 40 marks (again 50% of the total), includes three essay questions (EQs), labelled **Essay 1, Essay 2** and **Essay 3**, of which you should answer one.

The exam's assessment objectives

The examination has four **assessment objectives (AOs)**, which are set out in Table 2.

Table 2 The four examination assessment objectives

	Assessment objective 1	Assessment objective 2	Assessment objective 3	Assessment objective 4
Assessment objectives	Demonstrate knowledge and understanding of the specified content	Apply knowledge and understanding of the specified content to problems and issues arising from both familiar and unfamiliar situations	Analyse economic problems and issues	Evaluate economic arguments and evidence, making informed judgements

Answering data-response questions

Each of the Context data-response questions in Section A of the ECON 4 exam paper contains three sub-questions. These are listed as [01], [02] and [03] for the Global Context question, and [04], [05] and [06] for the EU Context question. The mark allocation for the three parts of each question is [01] and [04]: 5 marks; [02] and [05]: 10 marks; and [03] and [06]: 25 marks. The total mark for each data-response question is 40.

The ECON 4 data-response questions contain slightly more data than AS data-response questions in the ECON 1 and 2 examinations. The layout and structure of the question will be similar to the four data-response questions in the Questions and Answers section of this Guide. Each question is likely to contain two or three sets of data. With three data sets, the data will be labelled Extract A, Extract B and Extract C (for the Global Context question) and Extract D, Extract E and Extract F (for the European Union Context question). For each question, one set of data is likely to be numerical: for example, a line graph, a bar graph, a pie graph or a table. The other data set(s) will be text.

An incline of difficulty will be built into each DRQ, with the earlier parts of the question being the most straightforward. Typically, the key instruction words for each part of the DRQ will be as follows:

For [01] and [04]: Calculate the percentage change (in an aspect of the data shown in the first extract) and **identify** one significant feature of the data.

For [02] and [05]: Explain the meaning of (an economic term or concept), and **analyse** (an economic issue relating to the data in the text extracts).

For [03] and [06]: Evaluate (or possibly **Assess** or **Do you agree?**, together with **Justify your argument**).

Examiner tip
Make sure you take a calculator into the examination in order to perform the calculation required by the first part of the Context question.

The first two parts of the questions will be marked using an **issue-based mark scheme** which lists the marks that can be awarded for the particular issues (and associated development) that might be included in the answer. Only lower-level skills (meeting AOs 1 and 2) are tested in the first part of the questions. The higher-level skill of analysis is tested in the second and third parts of the questions, but evaluation is tested only in the last part, where it accounts for about 10 of the available 25 marks.

The final part of each DRQ differs from the earlier parts in three significant ways. First, and most obviously, it carries many more marks — 62.5% of the total marks for the question and 31.25% of the total marks for the whole paper. If you time the examination incorrectly and fail to develop your answer to the last part of the question beyond a cursory footnote, you will reduce considerably your chance of achieving a grade A, let alone an A*. Second, whereas the first two parts of the question should be answered quite briefly, you are expected to write an extended answer of at least two pages for the final part. Think of this as a full-blown but nevertheless concise essay. Third, as already indicated, higher-level skills of **analysis** and particularly **evaluation** are expected in your final answer.

A **levels of response mark scheme** containing five levels is used for the final part of each DRQ (and also the final part of each essay question in Section B of the ECON 4 exam paper). You must familiarise yourself with the 'levels' mark scheme and bear it in mind when you practise the last part of data-response questions and essay questions. The key command word (e.g. to evaluate or assess) must be obeyed for your answer to reach the higher Level 4 and Level 5 standards of attainment set out in the levels of response mark scheme. Take special note of the summaries of each level and the number of marks available for each level. These are:

Level 1: Weak with a number of errors (0 to 3 marks).

Level 2: Weak with some understanding (4 to 9 marks).

Level 3: Reasonable including some correct analysis but very limited evaluation (10 to 16 marks).

Level 4: Good analysis but limited evaluation (or reasonable analysis and reasonable evaluation) (17 to 21 marks).

Level 5: Good analysis and good evaluation (22 to 25 marks).

Your answer must evaluate the different arguments you set out, preferably as you make each argument. With many questions, discussion should centre on evaluating the advantages and disadvantages of a course of action mentioned in the question.

Whether or not you have evaluated each argument as you make it, always try to finish your answer with a conclusion, the nature of which should vary according to the type of discussion or evaluation required. The conclusion might judge the relative strengths of the arguments discussed, possibly highlighting the most important argument. With many questions it is more appropriate to conclude whether, on balance, the case for is stronger than the case against and to provide some credible and reasoned justification for your opinion.

Answering essay questions

You must select *one* essay question from a choice of three when answering Section B of the paper. The choice of question is obviously very important. Because the national economy accounts for approximately half the specification content, you should expect at least one essay question in which you apply macroeconomic theory, particularly the *AD/AS* macroeconomic model, to analyse and then evaluate specification topics such as growth, unemployment and inflation, and the causes and/or effects of monetary policy, fiscal policy and supply-side policy.

Likewise, because the international economy also accounts for approximately half the specification content, you should expect at least one essay question on international trade, patterns of UK or world trade, the balance of payments, exchange rates or globalisation.

Remember also that because of the Global Context and EU Context nature of the data-response questions, international issues probably account for over half the total exam paper (though both data questions focus on the *impact* of an international issue on the UK economy).

The essay questions are labelled Essay 1, Essay 2 and Essay 3. The two parts of Essay 1 are numbered [07] and [08]. The two parts of Essay 2 are numbered [09] and [10]. Finally, the two parts of Essay 3 are numbered [11] and [12].

The key instruction words for the two parts of each essay question are likely to be:

Explain

Evaluate (or possibly **Assess** or **Do you agree?**, together with **Justify your argument**)

As is the case with the first parts of the data-response question, the first part of the essay question tests the lower-level skills and assessment objectives of knowledge and application. The advice already given on how to answer the last part of the data-response questions is equally applicable to answering the second part of your chosen essay question.

The synoptic requirement of the ECON 4 examination

It is important to remember that the ECON 4 and ECON 3 examinations at A-level are **synoptic**. To understand what this means, you should compare the ECON 4 examination with the ECON 2 AS examination on The National Economy. Questions in the ECON 2 examination must test only knowledge and understanding of terms and concepts set out in the AQA Unit 2 specification. For example, an ECON 2 examination cannot contain a question which centres explicitly on how a market functions at the micro level (a Unit 1 topic), or on Globalisation (a Unit 4 topic).

However, ECON 4 exam questions can draw on specification topics in the Units 1, 2 and 3 specifications, though of course the main focus of a Context or essay question must be on Unit 4 specification content. To understand why this is so, you must understand the difference between vertical and horizontal synopticity. **Horizontal synopticity** requires the application of a Unit 3 microeconomic concept or theory to answer an ECON 4 macroeconomic question. By contrast, **vertical synopticity** requires the use of AS macroeconomic concepts and theories such as recession (in the Unit 2 specification) to answer ECON 4 macroeconomic questions.

It is important to remember the following points:

(1) *AD/AS* analysis is just as important for answering ECON 4 questions as it is for ECON 2 questions. Providing you covered the *AD/AS* macroeconomic model thoroughly at AS, you are unlikely to need any more knowledge of the model at A2. However, you must practise the skill of applying *AD/AS* analysis in a more sophisticated way.

(2) The main microeconomic theoretical model you learnt at AS (supply and demand and how markets function) crops up again in the Unit 4 specification in the context of floating exchange rates (just as it reappears in the Unit 3 topic of labour markets).

The four key skills

Knowledge and understanding

With respect to the two lower-order skills of **knowledge and understanding**, AQA requires you to show an awareness of economic terminology and theories relevant to the ECON 4 specification.

Application

Application requires the selection of an appropriate theory or set of theories from the intellectual toolkit stored in your brain to explain an issue or issues posed by the question. The issue may centre on the *causes* of an economic problem, or the *effects* of the problem. Application of your knowledge of events that are happening, or which have recently happened, in the economy is also required.

Analysis

For **Context** data-response questions, **analysis** requires selection of relevant information from the data source(s) and then the use of the selected information, perhaps as evidence, in your answer. Information in the data is there to provide a *prompt* or *prompts* for the answer. You should indicate which bits of the data you are using, mentioning the extract and the line numbers, without at the same time resorting just to 'copying out' sentences or numbers from the data. Data-response questions and essay questions also require you to use the economic theory set out in the ECON 4 specification (and, on occasion, the synoptic use of theories in the other three unit specifications) to analyse the economic problems and issues on which the question focuses.

Evaluation

Evaluation is the higher-order skill that separates good answers that earn an A*, A or B grade from those that at best reach Grade C. Evaluation is also the skill that students find it most difficult to display.

To evaluate, you need to demonstrate a critical approach to economic models and methods of enquiry: for example, the assumption that if the national economy is left alone without government intervention, free-market forces automatically produce economic growth and full employment. You should also demonstrate the ability to produce reasoned conclusions clearly and concisely, and to assess the strengths and weaknesses of economic arguments and limitations of the data in the question.

Competing theories or explanations often lead into evaluation. Evaluation can require you to explain why, in your view, some arguments or lines of reasoning are more important than others. Where appropriate, alternative and competing theories and viewpoints must be weighed up. The assumptions you are making should be stated, considered and sometimes questioned.

The effects of different types of government intervention in the national or international economy must be judged, sometimes exploring their possible 'knock-on' and 'feedback' effects elsewhere in the economy. Very often a part [04] or [08] asks for consideration of the **advantages** and **disadvantages** of, or the **costs** and **benefits** of, or the **case for** versus the **case against** a course of action mentioned in the question.

Good evaluation requires you to **prioritise** the evidence and arguments you introduce into your answer. One way to do this is to explain, when introducing each of the points or arguments you are making, whether in your view it is significant *always*, significant but *only under a particular set of assumptions*, or though relevant, rather trivial. When making such points, your answer must go beyond mere assertion, i.e. you must **justify** your arguments and use of evidence.

Finally, there are two different ways of evaluating, but in my view the first way is better than the second. My preferred way of evaluating is to assess the strengths and weaknesses of each argument as you bring it into your answer. Is it relevant always, or only some of the time when particular assumptions hold? If you organise your answer in this way, make sure that every time you introduce a new argument you start a new paragraph. It is also a good idea to leave a vacant line between paragraphs so that the examiner's eye is drawn to the fact that a new argument is being presented.

The second way to evaluate is to leave it all to the final concluding paragraph. At its worst, so-called evaluation presented in the concluding paragraph can boil down merely to a statement such as: *In my view, the case for is therefore stronger than the case against.* Unfortunately, such a concluding statement is not *evaluation*; it is unjustified *assertion*. Good evaluation in a concluding paragraph must always refer back to arguments used earlier in the answer, making a clear final judgement as to which arguments, if any, are most important. Perhaps the best approach to organising your answer is to combine the two methods of evaluation, namely evaluate each point as you develop your answer before concluding with a winding-up paragraph that presents an 'overview' or summary of the arguments you believe to be most important.

It is worth remembering that AQA draws students' attention to a significant distinction between **weak** and **strong** evaluation. Weak evaluation consists of little more than assertions unsupported both by evidence and by any analysis that accompanies it. By contrast, strong evaluation uses sound economic analysis to support conclusions being drawn, together with evidence from the real world.

Evaluation and levels of skill mark schemes

According to AQA mark schemes, however good the analysis, an answer devoid of evaluation cannot climb above **Level 2** in the mark scheme (4 to 9 marks). Likewise an answer with some evaluation but no analytical use of economic theory is generally constrained to Level 2. (Examiners sometimes apply the nickname 'a General Studies answer' to such answers.) A **Level 3** answer (10 to 16 marks out of the 25 available marks) must be a reasonable response, including some correct analysis but very limited or weak evaluation. A **Level 4** answer (17 to 21 marks) must include *either* some good and correct analysis but very limited evaluation, or reasonable analysis and reasonable evaluation. Finally, the highest level, **Level 5** (22 to 25 marks), requires both good analysis and good or strong evaluation, with final evaluation evident in a concluding paragraph.

Stretch and challenge

The questions set in ECON 4 and ECON 3 examinations offer you the opportunity of being 'stretched and challenged' in your responses to the questions you choose to answer. Stretch and challenge is designed to allow the brightest students the opportunity to demonstrate the full extent of their knowledge and skills.

According to AQA, the requirement to set questions in the ECON 4 and ECON 3 exams that stretch and challenge students is met by the parts of each of the data-response and essay questions that call for extended writing in the answers. These are the final parts of both the data-response questions and the essay questions. The higher skill levels (Levels 4 and 5) of the levels of skill mark scheme indicate the high expectations which students are required to meet in order to achieve high marks. The requirement for the questions set in the A2 examination papers to stretch and challenge are met by ensuring that mark schemes give due reward to students displaying the higher-level skills of analysis and evaluation in their answers to the last part of their chosen questions.

Achieving an A* grade

Stretch and challenge questions provide the opportunity to achieve an A* grade overall at A-level. Like the A* grade at GCSE, the A-level A* grade attempts to address the need for greater differentiation between the most able and the slightly less able students. The most able students should gain an A* grade, while the slightly less able should achieve the standard A grade. Most importantly, a very good performance at A2 is needed for an A* grade to be earned. A high mark at AS, accompanied by reasonable but not excellent performance at A2, may achieve an A grade, but not an A* in the overall A-level award that results from adding up the student's AS and A2 marks.

Understanding UMS marks

This section of the Guide explains how the 'raw' marks you earn for each A2 exam paper are converted to **Uniform Mark Scale (UMS) marks**.

Raw marks are the marks awarded by the examiners who mark your script. Each question has a maximum raw mark of 40, which, given the fact that you must answer two questions, means that the maximum raw mark for the ECON 4 exam paper is 80.

After all the scripts have been marked, and basing their decisions only on raw marks, a grade-awarding panel decides where the grade boundaries should be set for each of the A2 pass grades: A*, A, B, C, D and E.

After all the grade boundaries have been set as raw marks, e.g. 59 out of 80 for a Grade A and 66 out of 80 for an A*, each student's raw mark is converted into a UMS mark. UMS marks have the same grade boundaries — for all subjects and all unit exams. These are: **grade A*: 90%; grade A: 80%; grade B: 70%; grade C: 60%; grade D: 50%; grade E: 40%.** For each A2 exam paper, the raw marks required to achieve particular UMS grades vary a little from year to year. The two main factors which influence where the raw mark grade boundaries are set are as follows:

- A judgement made by the grade awarding panel as to whether the questions in the exam paper were relatively easy or difficult in comparison to questions set in previous examinations.
- Computer analysis of the marks earned at GCSE 2 years earlier by the cohort of students taking the A2 exam. Other things being equal, if computer analysis suggests that this year's students are more able (on average) than last year's students, the grade awarding panel may lower the total raw marks needed to achieve the different A2 grades. (The same grade-setting procedures are also used at AS.)

For A2 and the overall A-level, the **Uniform Mark Scale (UMS)** needed to gain an A grade and an A* grade are shown in Table 3. An average UMS mark of 90 for the ECON 4 and ECON 3 exam papers is required for an A* grade to be awarded — provided an overall UMS total of 320 out of the maximum mark of 400 is achieved overall for Unit exams (AS as well as A2).

Table 3 Uniform Mark Scale (UMS) requirements for grades A and A*

AS	Maximum mark	A2	Maximum mark
Unit 1	100	Unit 3	100
Unit 2	100	Unit 4	100
Total	200	Total	200
Grade A boundary	160	Grade A boundary	160
A-level (AS and A2)			
Total	400		
Grade A boundary	320		
A* requirement	320 overall, with 180 achieved at A2		

The exam questions in this Guide

The seven examination-style questions that follow shortly are designed to be a key learning, revision and exam preparation resource. There are four **data-response questions (DRQs)** and three **essay questions (EQs)**. The marks awarded for students' answers to these questions are raw marks and *not* UMS marks.

You can use the data-response and essay questions either as timed test questions in the lead-up to the examination or to reinforce your understanding of the specification subject matter, topic by topic, as you proceed through the Content Guidance. In this Guide, the data-response questions are numbered 1 to 4, but as explained earlier, in the AQA exam you will eventually sit, the two questions will be numbered **Context 1** and **Context 2**. The essay questions are numbered 5 to 7 here, though again, as explained earlier, in the exam they will be labelled **Essay 1**, **Essay 2** and **Essay 3**.

This section covering the data-response questions and essay questions also includes:
- a student's answer for each question
- examiner's comments on each student's answer explaining, where relevant, how the answer could be improved. These comments are denoted by the icon **ⓔ**.

A strategy for tackling the examination

(1) On opening the examination booklet, skim-read all the data-response and essay questions, but don't at this stage read the data extracts in the Context data-response question.

(2) Read both DRQs more fully, paying particular attention to the accessibility of the data and whether you can write a good answer to the final part of each question, the part that carries the most marks.

(3) After careful thought, make your final choice and spend about 55 minutes answering all the parts of the DRQ. Take account of the marks indicated in brackets for each sub-question when allocating the 55 minutes between each part of the question. Make sure you spend over half the time answering part [03] or [06].

(4) While answering the data-response questions, you will have been thinking subconsciously about the three essay questions you skim-read earlier. Again, you should choose the essay question primarily on the basis of the relative ease or difficulty of the second part of the three questions.

(5) For both your chosen questions, remember to obey the key instruction words at the beginning of each part of the question.

(6) Again, take account of the marks indicated in brackets for each sub-question when allocating the 55 or so minutes between each part of the question. Make sure you spend over half the time answering the second part of the essay question.

(7) In the last 10 minutes of the examination, read through your written answers to your chosen questions, checking and correcting mistakes — including spelling and grammatical mistakes.

How the ECON 4 exam paper is set: some implications

Very few students who sit AS or A2 exams give much thought to the process through which the exam paper they eventually answer in the summer (or possibly January) is set. For an AQA exam, the process starts about 15 months before the exam date, when the Principal Examiner who sets the paper first puts pen to paper (or these days, fingers to keyboard) to write the first versions of the questions that he or she wishes to set.

For many subjects, such as English Literature and French, the time lag between the setting and sitting of the exams is generally immaterial, since the exam specifications and question papers are relatively timeless and not influenced by recent events. But for current affairs orientated subjects such as Economics, the time lag does matter, particularly for the ECON 4 macroeconomic paper. For a data-response or Context question, the time period involved can extend to as much as 2 years before the exam. There are two reasons for this. First, Principal Examiners usually spend several months researching the data they wish to include in a question, and second, graphs are invariably several months old by the time they are selected for use in a question.

Meanwhile, events in the UK, EU and other global economies move on, leading to the possibility that an exam question will become significantly out of date by the time the exam paper is answered. To guard against this, the final part of a Context question is often worded: *Using the data and your economic knowledge, evaluate...*

Students are expected to use their knowledge of how the economy has changed in the months before the exam to write a more informed answer. A really good student often explains why the data in the question are out of date, before discussing how this is going to influence their response. A good example is provided by a recent European Union Context 2 question which asked students if they agreed with the view that the UK economy would benefit if the euro were to be adopted by the UK at some point in the future. By the time the paper was sat, the euro was on the cusp of the eurozone crisis. Not surprisingly, therefore, almost all the students who answered the question disagreed with the proposition in the question, but the best students fully justified their viewpoint.

Data-response questions
The global context

Question 1 **The impact of the global recession on the UK economy**

Total for this question: 40 marks

Study **Extracts A, B** and **C**, and answer **all** parts of the question which follow.

Extract A: Output forecasts for the world economy and for selected countries, 2009 and 2010

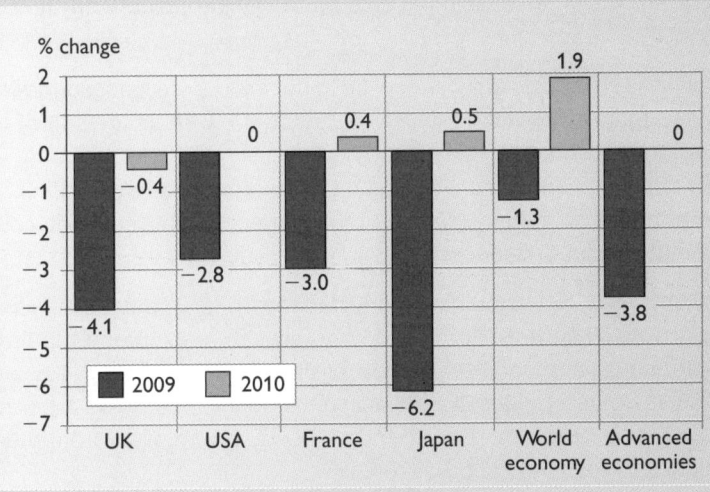

Source: IMF World Economic Outlook, April 2009

Extract B: The IMF's gloomy economic forecast

In April 2009, the IMF predicted that the UK would see its economy shrink by 4.1% in 2009, and by a further 0.4% in 2010. The IMF says this represents 'by far the deepest post-World War II recession', with an actual decline in output in countries making up 75% of the world economy.

The IMF believed that only a recovery in emerging market countries would propel   5
the world economy back into positive growth in 2010, albeit at a relatively weak rate of 1.9%.

Any recovery would be slower than in the past. There will be a smaller financial sector, with financing harder to come by than in the past, which will cramp economic growth. Rich countries such as the UK will face the burden of reducing their budget deficits which have soared during the crisis, at a time when their ageing populations mean they will have lower tax revenues.

10

Source: news reports, 2009

Extract C: The 'decoupling' debate

Before the onset of the global recession in 2008, many economists believed that the growing importance of emerging markets in countries such as China and India had 'decoupled' the economic cycles of countries such as the UK from the US economic cycle. As a result, they argued, recession or boom in the USA would no longer affect the UK economy significantly.

5

The counter-argument was that, through the process of globalisation, economies have become more intertwined through trade and finance. According to this view, other countries' economies have become more synchronized with the US cycle, not less.

So which view is right? The answer may lie in the middle. Recent economic history clearly shows that the recession which started in the USA as a result of the sub-prime mortgage scandal spread quickly to other countries, including the UK, through its effects on the world's financial system, American demand for imports, shrinkage of US investment in the rest of the world, and above all, the collapse of consumer and business confidence.

10

15

Yet at the same time, recession hardly affected the Chinese and Indian economies. After a relatively slight downturn, economic growth in China and India quickly returned to annual rates of GDP growth of close to 10%. Have China and India become the saviours of older industrialised economies? And has rapid recovery in China and India tipped the balance of economic power away from the EU and North America to south and southeast Asia?

20

Source: news reports, 2009

---

[01] Using Extract A, calculate the difference between the highest and lowest percentage changes in forecast output in 2009 for the various individual economies shown in the chart and identify one significant feature of the data.

(5 marks)

@ If you read through the first part of a Context data-response question pre-dating the 2012 exams, you will notice that the question always asked for identification of two significant points of comparison or two significant features displayed by the data. From January 2012 onwards, the nature of this part of the question has changed. The first part of a Context data-response question is likely to ask for a calculation, followed by identification of **one** significant feature of the data.

AQA A2 Economics

Up to 3 marks can be awarded for the calculation and up to 3 marks for identifying a significant feature, up to a maximum of 5 marks overall.

> **[02]** 'The IMF believed that only a recovery in emerging market countries would propel the world economy back into positive growth' (Extract B, lines 5–6). Explain the meaning of the term 'positive growth' and analyse how recovery in emerging market countries could propel the United Kingdom economy back into positive growth.
>
> (10 marks)

ⓔ Mark schemes for the second part of Context data-response questions indicate that 4 marks are available for explaining the meaning of a term in the second extract of the data and 6 marks are available for analysis of an issue or problem indicated by the text in the data.

> **[03]** Using the data and your economic knowledge, evaluate the view that **UK** economic performance is no longer highly dependent on how well the **US** economy is doing.
>
> (25 marks)

ⓔ Sixteen per cent of the total marks for the ECON 4 examination are given for the skill of evaluation, and almost all these marks are devoted to the final parts of the chosen data-response question and essay question. The key instruction is likely to be: evaluate, assess, or do you agree? Evaluation is the skill that students find most difficult and which is generally necessary if a grade A is to be earned, and it is certainly necessary if an A* grade is to be earned.

Student answer

[01] Since the 'world economy' is not an individual country, its data are excluded from my calculation. The USA experienced the smallest fall in forecast output (–2.8%) while Japan experienced the largest fall (–6.2%). The difference between the two forecast falls was therefore 3.4% **a**. A significant feature of the data is that it indicates all the selected countries in the chart were forecast to be in recession, but for the world economy as a whole, growth was expected to be positive **b** – presumably because of positive expected growth in emerging market economies such as China, which are not represented in the chart **c**.

ⓔ **5/5 marks awarded.** Although no statistical evidence from the data is provided for the 'significant feature' identified, the answer still earns full marks. **a** The precise and clearly explained calculation picks up all 3 of the available marks. **b** Although 3 marks are available for the 'significant feature', only 2 have been earned because of the lack of back-up evidence. **c** Explanation in terms of recession and emerging market countries does not count as statistical backup, so is irrelevant to the question.

[02] Positive growth can be defined as an increase in the level of real output over a particular time period, for example a year **b**. It can also be defined as an increase in the potential output an economy can produce, associated with an outward movement of the economy's production possibility frontier **a**. The term 'emerging market' is used to describe a newly industrialising (or industrialised) economy such as one of the so-called BRIC economies (Brazil, Russia, India and China). In the short run, though not necessarily in the long run, economic growth (or recovery from recession) is caused by an increase in aggregate demand **c**. This can result from a positive change in any of the components of aggregate demand shown on the right-hand side of the aggregate demand equation:

$$AD = C + I + G + (X = M)$$

$(X = M)$ is net export demand. If the UK's exports increase, while imports remain unchanged (or don't rise as much), export-led growth results. In the diagram below, the increase in net exports shifts the AD curve to the right, from AD_1 to AD_2. Output rises from y_1 to y_2, which means that short-run economic growth is taking place **d**.

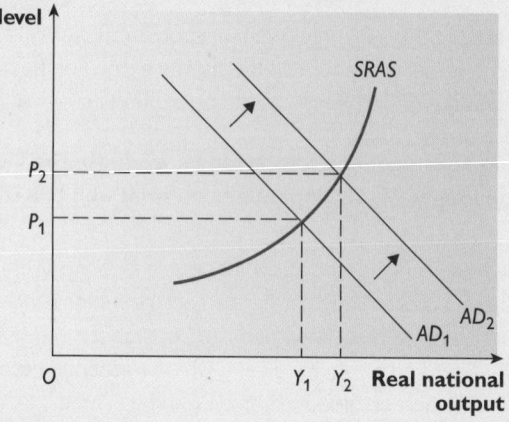

In the current world economy, the shift of regional economic power to emerging market economies means that demand for British goods, triggered by the fact that they recovered earlier from the 2008 recession than the UK, has meant that UK firms did indeed have the potential to benefit from export-led growth.

ⓔ **10/10 marks awarded.** This is an excellent answer that earns full marks. **a** The student provides a good, clear definition, though to some extent **b** he is mixing up the *measurement* of growth with the *definition* of growth. However, he is not penalised for this. Note how the student resists the temptation to evaluate the processes he describes. Part [02] (and part [05]) questions are about explanation and analysis, and do not require evaluation. **c** He introduces the distinction between short-run and long-run growth, but does not elaborate unnecessarily on the distinction. **d** The question does not require a diagram (and full marks can thus be earned without the inclusion of a diagram), but the AD/AS diagram adds to the overall quality of the answer.

[03] UK economic performance relates to how well (or badly) the British economy has recently performed (and is currently performing) with regard to the standard objectives of government macroeconomic policy. These are: reducing unemployment, achieving economic growth and higher living standards, controlling inflation, and achieving a satisfactory balance of payments on current account (or possibly a desired exchange rate for the economy). Good performance means that employment is growing (and unemployment is falling), maintaining or even improving the economy's sustainable growth rate (and reducing fluctuations around the trend growth rate associated with the economic cycle), achieving a satisfactory rate of inflation, and maintaining or improving the international competitiveness of UK businesses. Bad performance means the opposite.

There is a saying frequently trotted out in newspapers: when the USA sneezes, the rest of the world catches a cold. This saying alludes to the fact that for several decades, the US economy has been the largest and most dominant in the world, a major market for other countries' exports, and a source of foreign direct investment (FDI) flows as US companies such as Ford and Microsoft invest in factories, supermarkets (e.g. ASDA) and other businesses in countries such as Britain. When the American economy booms, the UK does well, benefiting from the demand from the huge American market for British exports, and the investment funds flowing from the USA to the UK. This induces export-led growth in the UK, and in terms of my earlier diagram (in my answer to part [02] **c**), this causes the *AD* curve to shift to the right, which promotes economic growth and reduces unemployment in the UK. (However, as the diagram also shows, it may also lead to excess demand pulling up the price level, i.e. demand-pull inflation.) If this happens, UK national performance deteriorates, at least in the sense of maintaining control over inflation **a**.

Just before recession hit the US economy in 2008, it became fashionable to ask: *have other countries 'decoupled' their economies from the US economy?* If decoupling had taken place, recession and boom in America might not lead inevitably to recession and boom in the UK and in other countries. It was argued that the size and rate of growth of emerging markets in BRIC countries and other 'less developed' countries might mean that they, rather than the USA, had emerged as the main markets and source of FDI for the UK economy.

In my view, the truth currently lies midway between the two extreme possibilities. There is plenty of evidence (Russians investing in English football clubs, the UK selling financial services to China) that the BRIC countries have become more important for the British economy and that they suffered less from the 2008 global recession. Yet by the opposite token, the recession (or at least the slowdown) suffered by virtually every country in the world in 2008 and 2009 emanated from the collapse in US demand and investment in other countries. This collapse was caused in large part by the 2007 'credit crunch', the US sub-prime mortgage problems, and the international financial crisis following the collapse of the US Lehman Brothers Bank in 2008. The rest of the world did indeed catch a cold as a result of crisis and recession in the USA. But recent events support the view that economic power is shifting from North America and west Europe to Asia. Asian countries are now much less willing to hold the US dollar in their currency reserves and to use the current account surpluses gained from exporting to the USA to supply America with a stream of savings to invest in the US economy **b**.

@ **24/25 marks awarded.** This is a rather discursive question that does not lend itself to straightforward application of the *AD/AS* model or to the use of production possibility curves and other diagrams to illustrate the points being made. However, in this case, the student has written an excellent answer that reaches the highest Level 5, which requires **a** good analysis and also **b** good evaluation. To reach Level 5 (and hence a mark between 22 and 25, with a midpoint at 24), a student has to display *most* but not all of the Level 5 qualities set out in the mark scheme. **c** At one point in the answer, to save having to repeat himself by drawing the same diagram twice, the student refers back to his answer to part [02]. From January 2012, this might not be a

wise strategy. From then on, the different parts of each question will be electronically assessed and marked by different examiners. The examiner marking the third part of your answer will not have read your answer to the second part. This means you should answer the sub-parts of each question (including the essay questions) without referring to what you have written in your answers to other parts of the question.

ℯ Scored 39/40: 97.5% = high grade A*

Question 2 **Trade, protectionism and the UK economy**

Total for this question: 40 marks

Study **Extracts A** and **B**, and then answer **all** parts of the question which follow.

Extract A: The UK and US current accounts, 1995–2010

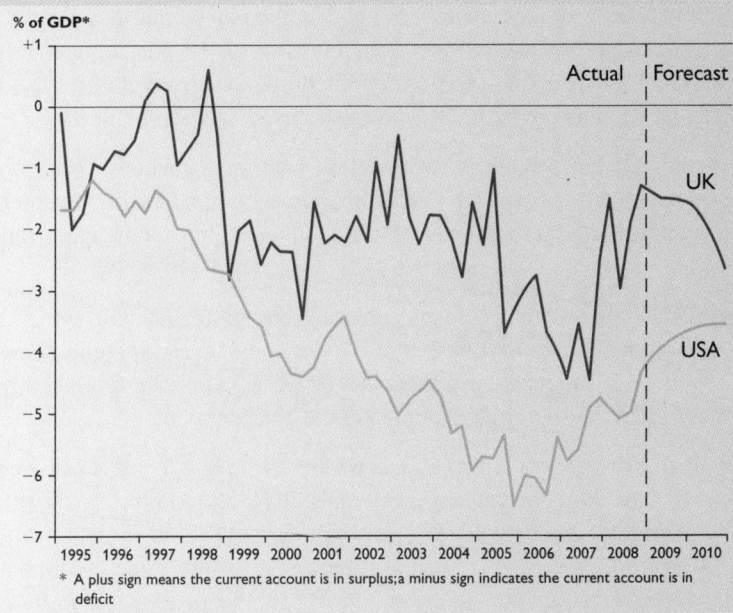

Source: official statistics, 2009

Extract B: Recession and the protectionist threat

Early in 2009, with UK industrial production suffering a year-on-year fall of 11.4%, some economists urged the UK government to subsidise struggling UK manufacturing firms. There had been plenty of action in rescuing banks, but little direct support to help manufacturing firms through the downturn.

But government subsidy for industry is, in essence, just another form of protectionism. However, when there was a synchronised global collapse in demand, protectionism could perhaps be excused as a way of keeping otherwise viable companies and skills alive until conditions recovered and they could begin operating normally again.

5

Yet as the recession which started in 2008 deepened, the danger grew of a   10
growing deluge of beggar-thy-neighbour protectionist measures, which will end
up destroying all the hard-won gains of wider trade liberalisation.

We draw much of our fear of protectionism from experience in the 1930s when
the USA raised import duties to record levels. Demand was by then already so
subdued that the new tariffs may not in truth have had the devastating economic   15
impact sometimes attributed to them. You can have as much in the way of import
duties as you like, but in circumstances where nobody is buying anything, they
are unlikely to help your own industries very much.

Few would seriously suggest history is about to be played out in quite the same
way this time. Hopefully, we've moved on a bit since then. Anything as crude as   20
what happened in the 1930s would require the whole framework of the World
Trade Organization to break down, and this doesn't seem at all likely.

But today, protectionism takes subtler, less obtrusive forms — subsidy, soft
loans, Buy American, British jobs for British workers, and so on. Yet there is a
growing weight of it, and this doesn't bode at all well for a recovery in trade and   25
economic activity.

Protectionism interferes with the process of creative destruction, which brutal
though it might be, is a core function of the economic cycle. Instead of out with
the old and in with the new, zombie manufacturers, kept alive on a steady drip-
feed of state aid, take their place alongside the zombie banks.   30

Philosophically, the UK government doesn't like the idea of protectionist policies
such as wage subsidies, but if everyone else is doing it, can they really afford to stay
out of the game? If it can be sold as a way of preserving skills, or perhaps helping
people retrain, then perhaps there might be a way. In any case, manufacturing
production and sales cannot keep collapsing at the present calamitous rate   35
without some eventual and fairly dire consequences for employment.

Attacks on free trade are on the increase. It's hard to believe it will end up as bad
as the 1930s, but we are fast sliding into a more protectionist world. Still, it ill
becomes Britain, which as an entrepôt nation trades widely with the rest of the
world and has more to lose than most from the closing up of national borders,   40
to introduce its own forms of protectionism in response to state subsidy on the
continent and Buy American policies in the USA.

Source: news reports, 2009

AQA A2 Economics

[01] Using Extract A, calculate the change in the US current account, as a percentage of US GDP, between the start of 1995 and the end of 2008, and identify one significant feature of the data.

(5 marks)

ⓔ Unlike in Question 1, where it is possible to calculate a precise figure, for this question it is difficult to read accurately the exact position of the line graphs at particular points on the horizontal axis. For this reason, examiners are granted a degree of flexibility. They are able to award full marks for calculations even if the answers are slightly above or below the numbers stated in the mark scheme.

[02] 'Protectionism interferes with the process of creative destruction, which brutal though it might be, is a core function of the economic cycle' (Extract B, lines 27–28). Explain what is meant by the term 'protectionism' and analyse this statement.

(10 marks)

ⓔ The question includes the term 'creative destruction' which may be unfamiliar to many students. However, Extract B provides an indication of what the term means. (From watching horror films, students may be more familiar with the word 'zombie', though as the answer below indicates, knowledge of this word does not necessarily improve an answer!) The extract makes at least two references to the 1930s. Questions will not test your knowledge of events in the UK economy extending back more than 10 years before the exam. Nevertheless, historical knowledge can be very useful for understanding modern events such as recessions.

[03] Using the data and your economic knowledge, evaluate the view that the UK economy can benefit more from free trade than from protectionism.

(25 marks)

ⓔ Sixteen per cent of the total marks for the ECON 4 examination are given for the skill of evaluation, and almost all these marks are devoted to the final part of the chosen data-response question. The key instruction is likely to be: evaluate, assess, or do you agree? Evaluation is the skill that students find most difficult and which is generally necessary if a grade A is to be earned, and it is certainly necessary if an A* grade is to be earned.

Student answer

[01] The US current account deficit stood at 1.8% of US GDP at the start of 1995. At the end of 2008 it stood at 4.5% of US GDP **a**. A significant feature of the data is that the UK current account was in deficit for almost all the actual and forecast period, but small surpluses were achieved in the middle of 1997 and 1998 **b**.

ⓔ **3/5 marks awarded. a** Only 1 mark has been awarded for the 'calculation', largely because no calculation has actually been made. The mark scheme does, however, allow 1 mark for what the student has written. **b** Two marks are awarded for the identified 'significant feature', but the third available mark is lost because no statistical backup has been provided. Overall the answer merits 3 marks.

[02] Protection means import controls. It can take the form of quotas which place a maximum limit on imports, and tariffs and export subsidies. A tariff or import duty makes imports more expensive in the home market, compared to prices of domestically produced goods. Export subsidies by contrast, make the country's exports cheaper abroad, compared to the prices of overseas produced goods **a**.

'Creative destruction' is a term used in the 1940s by the Austrian/American economist Joseph Schumpeter as a possible justification of very large firms, and indeed of monopoly. Schumpeter argued that monopoly power gave large firms the ability to become more efficient by investing out of current profit, then reducing prices and forcing rival firms out of business. Creative destruction allows new technologies, products and ways of producing products to replace old outdated methods and products. It is an element of improvements in dynamic efficiency. Schumpeter went on to argue that economic cycles (though he was analysing long cycles of about 60 years) also promote creative destruction. In the downturn of the cycle, weaker firms go to the wall in a deep recession and their assets are gobbled up and put to better use by the firms that survive the recession, fitter and leaner. By propping up and rescuing the weaker firms, protectionism prevents or slows down the process of creative destruction. Extract B uses the term 'zombie manufacturers'. This describes the firms that survive the recession that should have been allowed to die and disappear. In horror films, zombies are the 'walking dead', leaving their graves at night to haunt the living **b**.

ⓔ 9/10 marks awarded. Although the student displays a wealth of knowledge and evidence of background reading, her answer does not quite earn full marks. **a** Having gained 4 marks by explaining the meaning of protectionism in the first part of her answer, she needed to apply the concept in a more focused way in the second part of her answer. **b** However interesting it is, the description of a zombie should have been sacrificed to free space for more relevant economic knowledge.

[03] If in the distant past, the UK had remained a closed economy and refused to trade with other countries, the goods and services we now enjoy would be limited to those that could be produced solely from UK natural resources.

But in a world of completely free trade, in which domestically produced goods have to compete with those from other countries, imports enter the country priced at the ruling world price of P_W shown in the diagram below. This price is lower than the price that would exist (P_1) if imports were not allowed.

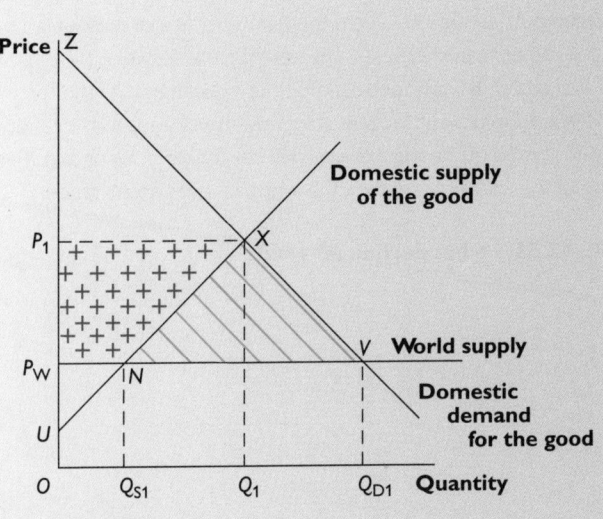

As a result of the fall in price, consumer surplus (a measure of consumer welfare) increases by the area bounded by the points $P_W VXP_1$. The area divides into two parts, shown on the diagram by the crossed and the striped areas. The crossed area shows a welfare transfer away from domestic firms to domestic consumers. The fall in the price from P_1 to P_W, brought about by lower import prices, means that part of the producer surplus domestic firms previously enjoyed now becomes consumer surplus. The consumers 'win' and the domestic producers 'lose' **a**.

Consumers also enjoy a further increase in consumer surplus, brought about by receipt of the striped area. Indeed, the total increase in consumer surplus gain exceeds the size of the welfare transfer from producer surplus to consumer surplus. The country as a whole enjoys a net welfare gain, equal to the striped area in my diagram **a**.

The obvious logic of my argument is that if Britain uses tariffs to protect domestic UK industries, part or all of the welfare gain I have just explained will disappear, becoming in fact a welfare loss **a**. Nevertheless various arguments can be used to justify import controls. Import controls, it is argued, can be used to protect infant industries while they grow. However, this justification is less appropriate for the UK than for a poor country trying to develop its industries from scratch. Rather, it might be more appropriate to argue that Britain should rightly try to protect sunset or geriatric industries (if there are any of them left) in older industrial regions from the competition of infant industries in countries in the poorer parts of the world **b**.

ⓔ **21/25 marks awarded. a** Although the student has used some very good analysis and has evaluated the arguments as she introduces them into her line of reasoning, I have placed the answer high in Level 4 rather than in Level 5. The descriptor for Level 4 (17 to 21 marks) is 'good analysis but limited evaluation'. **b** I have decided that the evaluation is a little too limited for Level 5 (good analysis and good evaluation), first because the answer ends a little bit up in the air, and second (and related to this point) because there is no conclusion drawing arguments together. Nevertheless, taking all the answers together, the script achieves an A* grade.

ⓔ **Scored 33/40: 82.55% = borderline A* grade**

The European Union context

Question 3 The impact of EU membership on UK macroeconomic performance

Total for this question: 40 marks

Study **Extracts A**, **B** and **C**, and answer **all** parts of the question which follows.

Extract A: UK trade with the EU and other groups of countries, exports and imports as percentages of UK totals, 1955 and 2009

UK trade with:	1955 Exports (%)	1955 Imports (%)	2009 Exports (%)	2009 Imports (%)
European Union	15.0	12.6	57.2	52.0
Other west European countries	13.9	13.1	4.4	8.5
North America	12.0	19.5	17.5	9.6
Other developed countries (excluding Russia and China)	21.1	14.2	4.1	4.0
Oil-exporting developing countries	5.1	9.2	5.2	2.5
The rest of the world	32.9	31.4	16.1	23.0

Note: due to rounding, the figures may not add up to 100%

Source: official statistics, 2010

Extract B: The European Union: a complete common market?

The European Union (EU) started life as a customs union in which goods could move freely between EU member states, without tariffs having to be paid. In 1993, the Union became a more or less full common market, in which services, labour and capital could, in theory, also move freely between member states.

But these freedoms are not complete. Indecision and then the inability to   5
impose uniform standards relating to goods, and distortions created by member governments favouring local suppliers, are two reasons why this is so. National governments still prevent foreign arms suppliers from competing in the supply of weapons, and the EU lacks a community-wide energy market. Competition is also discouraged in protected national energy markets from gas and   10
electricity supply companies located in other member countries. British energy

companies, for example, cannot take over similar French companies, but UK utility companies have been acquired by the French. The French government even prevented acquisition of a yoghurt manufacturer, deeming the business to be strategically important for the French economy. In Spain, Bank Santander acquired the Alliance & Leicester and Abbey banks, but British banks have found it difficult to take over Spanish banks.

15

Source: news commentary, 2009

Extract C: Macroeconomic performance in the UK and in the eurozone

Before 2004, the 15 countries then in the European Union were known as the EU-15. These are the developed countries, sometimes known as 'old Europe', located in western Europe. Twelve of these countries have abandoned their national currencies, using the euro instead. The 12 countries within the EU-15 that adopted the euro became known as the eurozone. The UK is an EU-15 country, but is not in the eurozone. From 2004 onwards, the European Union admitted a further 12 countries, expanding the EU-15 to become the EU-27. New entrant countries such as Poland and Estonia, which make up 'new Europe', are mostly in central Europe. Other countries such as Croatia and Turkey may join the EU in future years. Within the EU-27, 17 countries now use the euro.

5

10

Before 2008, the UK generally enjoyed a faster growth rate than the EU-15 and the eurozone. Though unemployment fell in the continental EU-15 countries, the UK unemployment rate was lower than in countries such as Germany and France. From 1998 to 2008, the eurozone unemployment rate was significantly higher than the UK rate. Indeed, at the time, the UK was benefiting from the largest and the longest-lasting fall in unemployment in its recent history.

15

Inflation rates were also generally falling in these years, lying within the acceptable range set by the UK government in Britain, and by the European Central Bank (ECB) in the eurozone. Things changed, of course, during 2007 and in later years. After a sudden surge in 2007 and early in 2008, the rate of inflation fell, leading to fears that problems induced by deflation would replace those associated with a rising price level. Unemployment began to grow in all EU countries as recession spread from the USA to Europe. With recovery from recession possibly beginning in 2009, growth is likely to remain depressingly weak and unemployment is likely to continue to grow, especially in the UK.

20

25

Source: news reports, 2009

[04] In 2009, the value of total UK exports was £217,673 million. Using Extract A, calculate the value of UK exports to the EU, and identify one significant feature of the data.   (5 marks)

e When performing a calculation, it is important to include in your answer the exact units of measurement that the question requires. In this case, although you are working in part from data measured in percentages, your final answer must be stated as millions of pounds.

[05] 'The European Union (EU) started life as a customs union in which goods could move freely between EU member states, without tariffs having to be paid' (Extract B, lines 1–2). Explain the meaning of the term 'customs union' and analyse possible benefits for a country joining a customs union.   (10 marks)

e The specification advises that the EU as a customs union should be considered in relation to the Single European Market (SEM). Although this question does not mention the SEM, you should familiarise yourself with its main features.

[06] Using the data and your economic knowledge, evaluate the view that the UK's macroeconomic performance benefits from Britain belonging to the EU, but not having adopted the euro.   (25 marks)

e This is an example of a type of European Union context question that often leads to very one-sided answers — usually rants against all things that are EU-related. Try to avoid doing this. To reach the higher Levels 4 and 5 when answering an [03] or [06] question, it is vital to consider carefully both sides of the issue(s) posed by the question.

Student answer

[04] UK exports to the EU were 52% of total exports which means their value was £113,190 **a b**. A significant feature of the data is that, with regard to both exports and imports as percentages of total UK trade, UK trade with the European Union grew, while trade with developing countries fell. Exports to EU countries grew from 15% of total UK exports in 1955 to 57.2% in 2008 **c**.

e **3/5 marks awarded. c** The student picks up all the available 3 marks for identifying a significant feature of the data, even though the feature identified is closely identified with the required calculation. **a** Unfortunately, however, no marks are earned for the calculation as the student has misread the question and used the import data rather than the export data. **b** He also makes the mistake of not stating that the number is measured in £ million.

[05] A customs union is a group of countries that sign a multilateral agreement, not only to abolish tariffs or import duties within the union, but to impose a common external tariff on imports from countries outside the union. Along with a free trade area, a customs union is a type of trading bloc. In a free trade area, internal tariffs are also abolished, but each country is free to impose its own tariffs on imports from non-members, i.e. there is no common external tariff in the case of a free-trade area **a**.

The main benefit of joining a customs union is to gain access to a larger market for the country's firms. The larger market results from tariff-free access to other countries' markets. The United Kingdom for example, with 60 million population, gains access to a market of over 300 million in the wider EU. This should enable domestic firms to enjoy much longer production runs and thus gain the benefits of economies of scale. Customs unions, along with other trading blocs, can be regarded as second-best outcomes. The best, which is unattainable because not enough countries agree on its creation, would be free trade throughout the world. There would be no tariffs at all, and hence no customs unions. Given the impossibility of achieving this, a customs union creates a limited area of free trade. Free-market economists generally argue that a free trade area is really the second best, and they relegate a customs union to third place position in the ranking of desirable outcomes **b c**.

🄔 **10/10 marks awarded. a** The explanation of the term 'customs union' earns all the available 4 marks. **b** The rest of the answer is certainly good enough to earn 6 marks for analysis (AQA mark schemes do, in fact, allow up to 8 marks for analysis). **c** The answer displays a succinct understanding of the nature of a customs union. If more marks and a longer time in which to answer the question were available, the student might have extended his answer by explaining that the benefits of a customs union depend on its size, whether it promotes internal trade in accordance with the principle of comparative advantage, and the extent to which it is trade creating rather than simply trade diverting.

[06] Macroeconomic performance is a measure of how well a country is doing in the world economy **a**. Joining the European Union, but not having adopted the euro as the currency used in the United Kingdom, means that Britain can gain the benefits of the single market within the customs union, but still implement a monetary policy which is in the UK's national interest, not a monetary policy decided by the European Commission in Brussels and the European Central Bank in Frankfurt.

The countries now in the eurozone are no longer free to implement independent monetary policies. The European Central Bank sets interest rates for the whole of the eurozone. Prior to the creation of the euro, the EU attempted to achieve convergence in the economic cycles of the initial 12 member countries. Without convergence, each country would have been in a different phase of its economic cycle, with some countries in recession or on the verge of recession, while others were in the recovery or boom phases of the economic cycle. Complete convergence, by contrast, means that every country is in the same phase of the economic cycle. In the event, only partial convergence was achieved. This meant (before 2008 when almost all EU countries, including Britain, were hit by recession) that a high interest rate was needed to dampen demand-pull inflationary pressures in the then fast-growing countries such as Ireland, while low interest rates were required to stimulate economic recovery or to ward off recession in other countries **b c**.

This led to the 'one size fits all' problem, which stems from the fact that these requirements are mutually exclusive. However, the political and economic power of Germany and France almost always overrode the requirements of countries on the periphery, such as Greece and Spain.

At the present time, the UK — though larger than Greece — is viewed in Brussels very much as a country on the periphery, semi-detached from mainstream Europe. In the early 2000s, just like Ireland, the UK economy was booming. Higher interest rates implemented by a Bank of England separate from the ECB were therefore needed to prevent a bubble economy from emerging. If Britain had previously adopted the euro, it would not have been able to raise interest rates to pursue the country's national interest.

However, the argument I have just summarised may not be consistent with the evidence about what has actually happened. In the early 2000s, the ECB, far from behaving in an inflationary way, was in fact criticised for being too cautious and deflationary when setting interest rates for eurozone countries. By contrast, within Britain, the Bank of England's monetary policy ignored the rapid rise in house and share prices that was taking place. It wrongly believed that inflation was under control as an asset price bubble was gathering steam. When the asset price bubble was pricked, as was inevitable, the UK economy fell into recession before the eurozone countries also suffered an economic downturn **d**.

In conclusion, therefore, I don't agree that UK macroeconomic performance has benefited from the country not having adopted the euro. However, being outside the eurozone does mean that the UK is free to devalue the pound's exchange rate in order to try to gain a competitive advantage for Britain's exports. Eurozone countries such as Spain and Italy can't devalue their currencies because their national currencies no longer exist. There may be some benefits from not having adopted the euro, but I think the costs of remaining outside the eurozone are greater **e**.

e   19/25 marks awarded. a If you refer back to the student's answer to part [03] of Question 1 on pages 78–79, you will see how you should start the answer to a question which mentions economic performance, be it national economic performance or macroeconomic performance. This answer, by contrast, while mentioning macroeconomic performance, says very little about what the term means. Consequently, the explanation does not really offer a platform on which to develop the answer.

But despite this rather woolly first sentence, *most* of the rest of the answer is good. **b** The discussion about the benefits and costs of the UK adopting the euro is impressive. **c** However, overall, the answer is lopsided because it provides only a very brief discussion, towards the beginning of the answer, of the benefits (and costs) of EU membership (as distinct from euro adoption and membership of the eurozone). For this reason, I have decided to place the answer at the middle of Level 4 (reasonable analysis and evaluation), which covers the mark range 17 to 21. **d** The student does make some good evaluative points, but as I have explained, the analysis is a bit too narrow to justify a higher mark. **e** Additionally, there is a rather limp conclusion.

e   Scored 32/40: 75% = sound A grade

Question 4 Fiscal policy and government borrowing in the UK and the EU

Total for this question: 40 marks

Study **Extracts A**, **B and C**, and then answer **all** parts of the question which follow.

Extract A: National debt as a percentage of GDP, 2003 to 2014

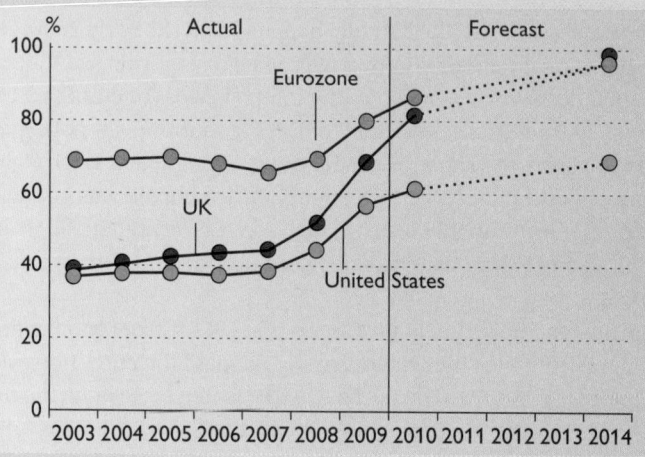

Source: official statistics, 2009

Extract B: Government borrowing and debt, in the UK and the EU

The European Union's Stability and Growth Pact (SGP) requires that *all* EU member countries agree to limit their budget deficits as a proportion of GDP. In normal times *all* members of the European Union (and not only the eurozone members) are meant to aim for balanced budgets, or small budget deficits or surpluses. Governments that run fiscal deficits bigger than 3% of GDP are supposed to take swift corrective action. If a eurozone country breaks the 3% limit for more than 3 years in a row, it becomes liable to fines of billions of euros. These provisions are meant to be so intimidating that no government dares breach the 3% rule, but in practice, it has not worked out like that.

Governments have to borrow to finance a budget deficit, and government borrowing adds to government debt (the National Debt). By the end of 2009 UK government borrowing was growing at a much faster rate than borrowing in other EU countries. This may pose huge problems for the UK economy in future

5

10

years. Action must therefore be taken to reduce the size of UK government borrowing, not so much to meet the Stability and Growth Pact's rules, but to save the British economy.

15

Source: academic research paper, 2009

Extract C: Should the fiscal stimulus be ended?

Alistair Darling, the Labour government's Chancellor of the Exchequer, has warned that the world could be dragged into a double-dip recession if other governments stop using an expansionary fiscal policy to stimulate their economies. He said he would oppose moves by France and Germany to end the fiscal stimulus policies they had cautiously adopted to try to spend their economies out of recession.

5

Britain's recovery from recession is lagging behind France and Germany, who both returned to economic growth in mid-2009. Germany's Angela Merkel and French President Nicolas Sarkozy are now keen to end the multibillion euro fiscal stimulus packages that are credited with easing some of the pain of the recession, but which have also sent government borrowing soaring. But Labour's Chancellor is determined to fight those who believe the crisis is over. In 2009 the government cut VAT, at least until January 2010, pumped billions into failing banks, and authorised the Bank of England to engage in a quantitative easing programme to try to restore normal banking conditions. Economists now believe that the cost in UK government borrowing for this year alone will exceed Darling's target of £175 billion.

10

15

The UK Chancellor's views are echoed by some of his counterparts around the globe. Yesterday Jean-Claude Juncker, the chairman of eurozone finance ministers, said that 'while the worst is over for the time being, governments should be wary of withdrawing fiscal stimulus measures too quickly'.

20

Source: news reports, 2009

---

[04] Using Extract A, calculate the difference between the UK's national debt as a percentage of GDP and that for the whole eurozone at the end of 2008. Then identify one significant feature of the data over the period shown.

(5 marks)

ⓔ The calculation required by the question must relate solely to the date specified in the question (the end of 2008), but you can select and explain *any* feature of the data — providing the examiner agrees with you that your chosen feature is *significant*.

[05] 'Governments have to borrow to finance a budget deficit, and government borrowing adds to government debt' (Extract B, lines 10–11). Explain the meaning of the term 'budget deficit' and analyse the relationship between government borrowing and government debt.

(10 marks)

ⓔ The 'explanation' part of the question is testing synoptically the knowledge you learnt at AS, namely knowledge of budget deficits. The 'analysis' part is more demanding, though is easier to understand if you remember that government borrowing is a 'flow' which, if not paid back, adds to the 'stock' of debt, in this case the National Debt. The National Debt is not mentioned in the specification, so you are not expected to know the term.

[06] Extract C, lines 4–5, states that France and Germany were likely to end their fiscal stimulus policies, aimed to get their economies out of the recession, before the UK took similar action. Using the data and your economic knowledge, discuss whether the UK's fiscal policy should always be different from the fiscal policies of members of the eurozone. (25 marks)

ⓔ This question is of course now out of date. **All** countries have been forced by the emergence of the sovereign debt problem to abandon fiscal stimulus policies adopted in the 2008–09 recession.

[04] The UK's debt was 40 while the eurozone's debt was about 68 at the end of 2008 **a**. A significant feature of the data is that Britain's national debt level was higher than US national debt throughout the period from 2003 to 2014, except at the beginning of 2003 when they were about equal **b**.

ⓔ **0/5 marks awarded.** This answer is bad on a number of counts and earns no marks. **a** The student shows no understanding of the meaning of percentage data. Related to this, the units of measurement are not mentioned in the calculation. **b** And her chosen 'significant' feature is complete nonsense. It is not possible to deduce from the data themselves that the UK's national debt was larger than US debt. It was larger as a *percentage* of total UK debt, but not as an absolute total.

[05] A budget deficit occurs when the total value of imports exceeds that of exports **a**. Government borrowing takes the form of selling National Savings certificates and premium bonds to people like you and me. We buy them because we think they are safe, but you can usually get a better deal from a building society such as the Nationwide **b**. Government debt is the same as government borrowing; there is no other relationship between the two **c**.

ⓔ **0/10 marks awarded.** Again this answer earns no marks. **a** The answer starts with a common error made by students: confusing the government's budgetary position (relating G to T) with the country's current account position on the balance of payments (represented by X and M). If you make this mistake in an exam and write about the wrong sort of deficit, you will not earn any marks. **b** However, even when it eventually focuses on government finances, the rest of the answer is no better. It drifts into irrelevance. **c** The student fails to analyse how government borrowing is a flow per time period (e.g. a year) that finances the government's budget deficit ($G > T$). She could also analyse how the flow of new borrowing, assuming that borrowing is not paid back during the course of the year, adds to the stock of government debt.

[06] Fiscal policy can be defined as the use by the government of the fiscal policy instruments, government spending and taxation, to try to achieve government policy objectives such as full employment, economic growth and control of inflation.

In 2008 and 2009 continental EU countries such as Germany and France (as well as the UK) were in recession. There was a lack of aggregate demand, and unemployment grew to approach 3 million in the UK by the end of 2009. (Some economists said that the true figure was much larger, possibly as high as 5 million as lots of the unemployed were not registered on the claimant count and the total number was underestimated by the Labour Force Survey.) Because there was general agreement that most of the unemployment was cyclical, resulting from deficient aggregate demand, many economists, particularly Keynesians, argued that governments and central banks should undertake a massive expansion of aggregate demand. They believed that if this did not happen, the already-severe recession would become a full-blown depression that could even be worse than the Great Depression of the 1930s.

Two main types of policy were called for. These were quantitative easing and very low interest rates (in monetary policy) and a huge fiscal stimulus (in fiscal policy). Quantitative easing increases the money supply. It was hoped that when people spend this money in a stagnant economy, aggregate demand increases and shifts the economy from point X to point Z in my production possibility diagram.

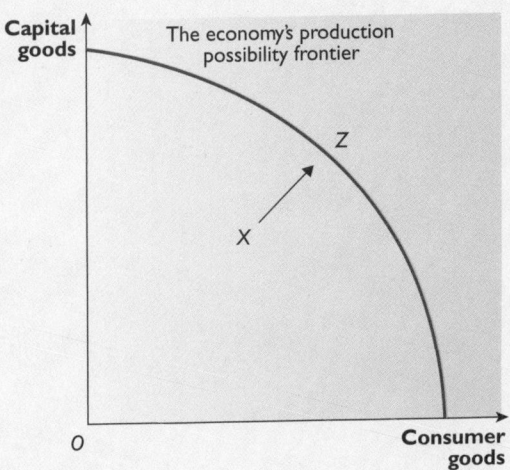

According to Keynesian economists, the monetary policy of quantitative easing and low interest rates should work in tandem with the fiscal stimulus brought about by tax cuts and massive increases in government spending. Again, it was hoped that the fiscal stimulus would help to shift the economy towards full employment at point Z on my diagram.

At the beginning of the recession in 2008, there was considerable agreement among eurozone member countries, and also in the UK, that such 'panic' policies should be undertaken. However, this consensus soon broke down.

Germany and France decided that a massive fiscal stimulus was not required, possibly because their recessions were shallower and they were already beginning to see 'green shoots' of recovery, while the UK economy continued to languish. Even in Britain, leading Conservative politicians David Cameron and George Osborne broke ranks with the Labour government and said that government spending should be cut and not raised, in order to get the public finances out of the giant hole into which they were slipping. When elected into power in 2010, they did precisely this.

🄴 **16/25 marks awarded.** This is much better than the student's answers to the earlier parts of the question, reaching the top of Level 3 (an adequate answer with some correct analysis but very limited evaluation). Nevertheless, because the answer is rather limited, it does not reach Level 4. Despite the instruction in the question, the student makes no explicit reference to the data and is really failing to answer the set question. The mention of Germany's Angela Merkel and French President Nicolas Sarkozy in relation to fiscal stimulus policies in Extract C provides an obvious prompt to develop a line of reasoning. A Level 4 or 5 answer might also discuss the implications of the EU's Stability and Growth Pact (described in Extract B), explaining how the pact supposedly limits the freedom of eurozone countries to set their own fiscal policies, while the UK, being outside the eurozone, enjoys more freedom.

🄴 **Scored 16/40: 40% = D/E grade boundary**

Essay questions

Question 5 Inflation and deflation

[07] Explain different possible causes of inflation. (15 marks)

(e) It is always a good idea when answering the first part of an essay question to define precisely any key terms in the question, in this case 'inflation'. For essays, mark schemes usually grant 2 marks per relevant definition, and the mark scheme may reward two definitions.

[08] 'Since the costs of inflation exceed the benefits of inflation, deflation must be good for the economy.' To what extent do you agree with this view? Justify your answer. (25 marks)

(e) With this type of question, it is wise not to agree wholeheartedly, or by the opposite token to reject completely, the question's central assertion. Instead, it is best to adopt an 'it all depends' or an 'on the one hand this, on the other hand that' approach, also known as 'sitting on the fence'. However, if you adopt this strategy, to earn a high mark you must use evidence to justify your conclusion.

Student answer

[07] Inflation is defined as a continuing or persistent rise in the average price level, or a continuing fall in the value of money **a**. For example, when the annual inflation rate is 3%, goods which cost 103p today would have cost £1 a year ago. The rate of inflation is measured by the annual rate of change in the retail prices index (RPI), or these days as far as the Bank of England is concerned, the annual rate of change in the consumer prices index (CPI). The Bank of England currently implements monetary policy to try to achieve the 2% inflation rate target, measured by the CPI, set by the government **b**.

There are two main causes of inflation, excess demand and rising production costs. The former is known as demand-pull inflation and the latter as cost-push inflation. Both are illustrated in the diagrams.

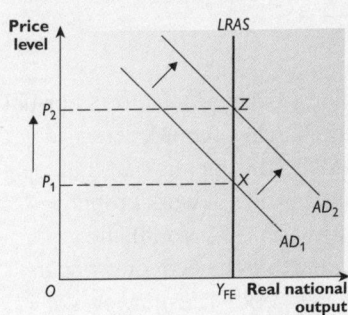

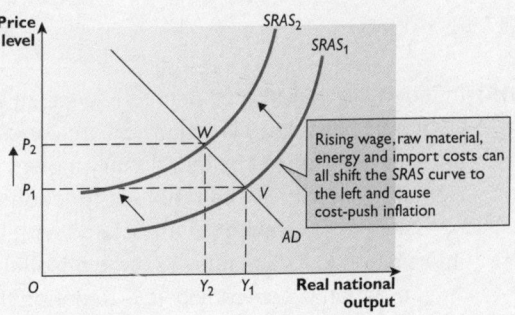

In the left-hand diagram, one of the components of aggregate demand ($C + I + G + (X - M)$) has increased, for example consumption spending (C). This causes the aggregate demand curve to shift to the right, from AD_1 to AD_2. I am assuming that the economy is producing on its vertical long-run aggregate supply curve labelled $LRAS$. This means there is no spare capacity in the economy. Given this situation, the increase in aggregate demand creates excess demand. Consumers are spending more, but real output cannot increase in the short run. With output remaining at its full-employment level (y_{FE}), something has to give. The thing that gives is the price level, which is pulled up by excess demand. Macroeconomic equilibrium moves from point X on the diagram to point Z **c**.

As the right-hand panel of my diagram indicates, cost inflation, by contrast, is caused by an increase in one or more of the factors shown in the 'box' on the diagram, wage costs, raw material costs, energy costs (especially oil costs) and import costs. When any of these increase, then assuming the cost increase is not offset by a cost decline originating elsewhere in the economy, the short-run AS curve shifts upwards and to the left, from $SRAS_1$ to $SRAS_2$. Macroeconomic equilibrium moves from point V on the diagram to point W.**c**

ⓔ **11/15 marks awarded. a** While it is always best to start the first part of an essay question by defining key concepts in the wording of the question, this student then does what many students often do when answering questions on inflation. **b** In his first paragraph he just writes what he knows on inflation, including material that is not relevant for answering the set question. **c** Fortunately, the drift is not too great, and focus is restored in the following paragraphs.

This question could very well have been set at AS rather than at A2. At AS, this answer would have been quite sufficient to earn full marks. However, at A2 more depth of analysis is required. The student might have brought in the monetarist explanation of inflation and the role of the money supply when explaining demand-pull inflation. He might also have explained how the government's budget deficit and public sector expenditure can create excess demand for output. Likewise, he should have developed his explanation of cost-push inflation: for example, by explaining that when wages increase at a faster rate than labour productivity, not only might excess demand result, but employers' real costs of production increase. Faced with increased real production costs, firms that enjoy a degree of monopoly power raise their prices so as to maintain their profit margins.

[08] Inflation is generally considered bad for an economy because it distorts normal economic behaviour. When prices are constantly changing, consumers are likely to be confused by inflationary 'noise'. Basically, this means that the signalling, incentive and rationing functions of prices do not work properly because the price changes associated with inflation send out confusing information **a**. As a result, resource misallocation within the economy occurs.

If inflation is generally bad, is deflation therefore good? The answer is generally yes, providing people can maintain their money incomes. If money incomes remain the same, or even grow, then people inevitably become better off in real terms when average prices fall **a**. Since one of the most important objectives of a government's macroeconomic policy is to raise real incomes in order to improve living standards, it follows that falling prices must be good **b**.

e **12/25 marks awarded. a** Although the student introduces and explains two good arguments into his answer, that is all he does. A wider range of arguments need to be considered: for example, drawing on the benefits of inflation, as well as other costs, which are summarised on pages 29–31 in the Content Guidance section of this Guide. Much more needs to be said about deflation. The standard case against deflation is that it is associated with recession and a depressed economy. There is a danger that an excessive reduction in aggregate demand designed to bleed inflation out of the economic system will do more harm than good to the economy. According to this line of reasoning, it is better to live with low but stable inflation as the necessary spin-off of a growing economy accompanied by consumer and business optimism. The flip side to this argument is that an apparently acceptable rate of inflation can quickly mutate into a high, accelerating and damaging inflation rate which is beyond the control of the government and central bank, except at the cost of accepting a massive recession and high unemployment.

b There are a number of other arguments the student might have considered. He could have debated the possibility that falling prices create incentives for people to postpone spending decisions, thus exacerbating deficient aggregate demand. Perhaps the most deep-seated approach would be to distinguish between a 'good' deflation and a 'bad' deflation. In a 'bad' deflation, average prices fall as a result of recession and a collapse of aggregate demand. By contrast, a 'good' deflation is brought about by increases in productivity and productive efficiency that result, in part, from technical progress. Falling real production costs throughout the economy cause the *LRAS* curve to shift to the right and the average price level to fall.

I have decided to place this answer towards the bottom of Level 3 (an adequate answer with some correct analysis but very limited evaluation). Apart from writing too narrow an answer, the student has insufficiently debated the issue posed by the question: namely, given the assumption that the costs of inflation exceed the benefits, can it be concluded that deflation is good for the economy?

e **Scored 23/40: 57.5% = B/C grade boundary**

Question 6 Supply-side macroeconomic policy

[09] Explain how supply-side economic policies can be used to improve productivity, efficiency and national economic performance.

(15 marks)

ⓔ This question asks students to explain the effect of supply-side economic policies on three related issues. A good answer must consider all three. Note also the word 'can' in the question. This provides some leeway in your answer for perhaps considering less obvious supply-side policies, but avoid drifting into demand-side policies.

[10] Assess the view that supply-side policies should be regarded as more important than demand-side policies in the macroeconomic management of the UK economy.

(25 marks)

ⓔ In contrast to the first part of this question, demand-side policies such as expansionary and contractionary fiscal and monetary policy, used to shift the *AD* curve, must be brought into the answer.

Student answer

[09] Supply-side policies are the set of government policies that aim to increase labour productivity and to make markets function more efficiently and competitively **a**. Supply-side policies thus aim to increase the economy's ability to produce within the country the goods and services that people want, and also goods that are in demand in export markets. Labour productivity is output per worker, and national economic performance is measured by the extent to which economic growth is achieved, jobs are created, inflation is controlled, and the country's industries are competitive in world markets **b**.

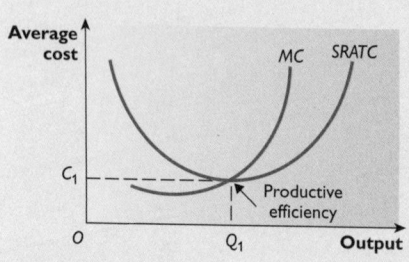

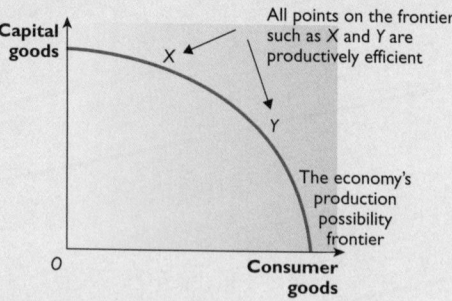

There are a number of different types of economic efficiency. Two of the most important are productive efficiency and allocative efficiency. Productive efficiency occurs when average costs of production are reduced to the minimum possible. The productively efficient level of output for a firm is shown in the left-hand diagram and for the whole economy in the right-hand diagram.

Allocative efficiency requires that resource misallocation is got rid of, or at least minimised. It requires the signalling and incentive functions of prices to function well in order to create the conditions in which scarce resources can be allocated between competing uses in ways which improve economic welfare throughout society **b**.

>   At the macroeconomic level, perhaps the main supply-side policies are
>   those that aim to increase personal incentives in labour markets. Supply-
>   side economists believe that high rates of income tax and the overall burden
>   of taxes upon taxpayers create disincentives in the labour market. The
>   disincentives destroy the will to work, which, by reducing national income as
>   taxation increases, then reduces the government's total tax revenue.
>
>   If the government wishes to increase total tax revenue, it must cut tax
>   rates rather than increase them. A reduction in tax rates creates the incentives
>   needed to stimulate economic growth. Faster growth means that total tax
>   revenue increases despite the fact that tax rates are lower. Arguably the effect is
>   reinforced by a decline in tax evasion and avoidance, as the incentive to engage
>   in these activities reduces at lower marginal tax rates **c**.

ⓔ **12/15 marks awarded. a** To repeat my earlier advice, it is always a good idea to define
key concepts in the question. **b** However, this student spends too long on definitions, given that
a maximum of 4 marks are available for explaining the meaning of key terms. The student should
have devoted more of her answer to addressing the issue posed by the question: namely, how
supply-side policies may improve productivity, efficiency and national economic performance. **c**
While the answer links supply-side fiscal policy to national economic performance, explanation of
how supply-side policies might improve productivity and efficiency is needed for full marks to be
earned.

[10] Whereas demand management policies are essentially short term, supply-side
policies try to improve the economy's ability to produce in the medium and long
term, perhaps many years in the future. Supply-side policies, which are often
microeconomic rather than macroeconomic, aim to increase the efficiency
and competitiveness of all the markets in the economy: goods markets (or
product markets), the labour market and financial markets. The expression
'first the pain, and then the gain' captures a key element of supply-side policy
a. By making it easier for firms to hire and fire workers, and by removing state
support for industry, supply-side policies initially increase personal risk and
insecurity. However, by creating incentives to be entrepreneurial, to supply
labour, to save and to invest, supply-side policies may eventually improve
long-run economic performance. Successful supply-side policies increase the
economy's trend rate of growth, illustrated in my diagram below through the
$LRAS$ curve shifting to the right from $LRAS_1$ to $LRAS_2$ **b**.

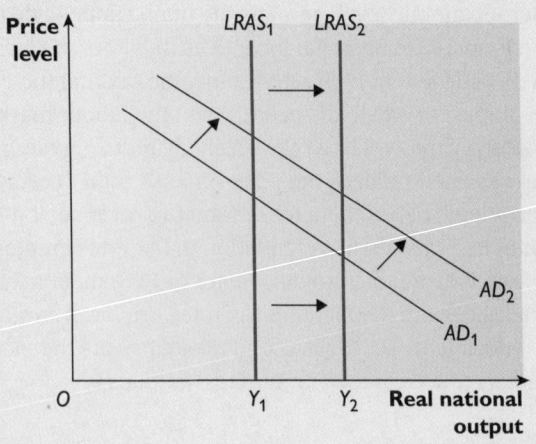

However, my diagram also shows the aggregate demand curve shifting to the right from AD_1 to AD_2. This illustrates the last argument I wish to make, namely that the role of aggregate demand should not be ignored when advocating the case for supply-side policies. Because supply-side policies increase the total level of output that the economy can produce, successful supply-side policies mean that aggregate demand must also increase so as to absorb the extra output. Without the required increase in aggregate demand, economic growth might be brought to a stuttering halt because of insufficient spending in the economy. Free-market economists argue that free-market forces automatically generate the extra demand required to absorb extra output. However, Keynesian economists disagree, arguing that if people save too much of their incomes, the incentive to produce the extra output may not be there. In this situation, demand-side policies (expansionary fiscal and/or monetary policy) may be needed to generate the extra demand required **c**. If this is the case, used wisely, demand-side and supply-side policies are best regarded as complementary policies rather than as substitutes for each other. Neither policy should be regarded as always more important than the other **d**.

ⓔ **23/25 marks awarded.** This is an excellent answer that shows **a** a deep understanding of supply-side economics and supply-side policies, together with **b** an implied understanding of demand-side policies. **c** Analysis and **d** evaluation are very good throughout the answer, which is completed by a final paragraph that justifies the conclusion drawn. It would be hard to see how a better answer could be written amongst the stresses and strains of the exam room, and given the time constraint. However, some discussion of the respective weaknesses of both sets of policies would have added to the answer. This is definitely a Level 5 answer; I have awarded 23 marks.

ⓔ **Scored 35/40: 87.5% = good A* grade**

Question 7 The benefits and costs of globalisation

[11] Explain the main features of globalisation. (15 marks)

e As always, when answering the first part of an essay question (or the second part of a Context question) you should start your answer by defining the key concept in the question — in this case, globalisation. At the very minimum, you should try to identify at least three key features and explain each in some detail. It is probably unwise to bring in too many features, if all you then do is write a single sentence for each.

[12] Evaluate the view that everybody must benefit from globalisation. (25 marks)

e The word 'must' is a key word in this question. When words such as 'must', 'always', 'solely' and 'inevitably' appear in the last part of an essay or Context data-response question, your answer will not score highly if it agrees or disagrees 100% with the central assertion in the question. It is always best in your answer to adopt an 'it all depends' approach.

Student answer

[11] Globalisation is the name given to the processes that integrate all or most of the world's economies, making countries increasingly dependent upon each other **a**. Globalisation has been made possible by improvements in information and communication technology (ICT), as well as by developments in more traditional forms of technology. These include massive improvements in passenger air flights and containerisation, which have greatly reduced the cost of shifting people and freight around the world. Examples of globalisation include service industries in the UK dealing with customers through call centres in India, and fashion companies designing their products in Europe, making them in southeast Asia and finally selling most of them in North America.

Two of the main features of globalisation are:

The growth of international trade and the reduction of trade barriers — a process encouraged by the World Trade Organization (WTO). Globalisation involves the liberalising or freeing-up of world trade. As a result of successive rounds of tariff reduction started in the 1940s, import duties have fallen. This allows specialisation and trade to take place in accordance with the principle of comparative advantage, which in turn increases production and consumption possibilities for most of the different countries in the global economy.

Greater international mobility of capital and to some extent of labour. Globalisation enables the movement of capital from developed economies to poor economies. In theory it also leads to labour mobility in the opposite direction. However, immigration controls slow down the movement of labour from poor to rich countries. Nevertheless, in recent years illegal immigration into developed economies has occurred because rich countries have informally encouraged migrants to fill the relatively low-paid jobs rejected by their own citizens **b**.

In summary, some of the other features of globalisation are:

- a significant increase in the power of international capitalism and multinational corporations (MNCs) or transnational companies
- the deindustrialisation of older industrial regions and countries, and the movement of manufacturing industries to newly industrialised countries (NICs)
- more recently, the movement of internationally mobile service industries, such as call centres and accounts offices, to NICs
- a decrease in governmental power to influence decisions made by MNCs to shift economic activity between countries **c**.

ⓔ 13/15 marks awarded. The student clearly understands what globalisation is, **a** defines the concept and **b** explains two of the main features of the process. **c** Having done this, he then lists four other characteristics of globalisation but does not explain them. Overall, his answer falls just short of full marks, which require explanation of a third feature of globalisation. He might have explained a feature of recent globalisation: namely, newly emerging economies such as China and India investing in older developed economies such as the UK.

Student answer

[12] Free-market economists generally support globalisation and regard its growth as inevitable. They argue that the benefits of further global economic integration, which include the extension of political freedom and democracy as well as the economic benefits of more production and higher living standards, significantly exceed the disadvantages, such as the destruction of local cultures. However, opponents argue that globalisation is a respectable name for the growing exploitation of the poor, mostly in developing countries, by international capitalism and US economic and cultural imperialism **b**.

For its critics, low-paid workers in sweatshops, farmers in the developing world being forced to grow genetically modified crops, the privatisation of state-owned industry to qualify for IMF and World Bank loans, and the growing dominance of US corporate culture and multinational companies symbolise what is wrong with globalisation. According to this view, which I hold myself, globalisation has led to a 'McDonaldisation' or 'Coca-Colonisation' of significant parts of the world's economy. This has involved and continues to involve the destruction of local and national products, identities and cultures by US world brands. The opposite process of 'glocalisation' or local action is needed to prevent or offset the damage done by globalisation to vulnerable local cultures. Supporters of globalisation counter by arguing that people in the rest of the world demand US products because they consider them superior to traditional local produce **b**.

Another feature of globalisation that has been criticised is the alleged treatment of local labour by multinational corporations. Companies such as Nike have been accused of selling trainers and footballs in developed countries such as the UK at prices far above the cost of raw materials and the low wages paid to Third World labour making the goods. But in response, the multinationals argue that the low wages they pay far exceed the local wages paid by firms indigenous to the countries in which they manufacture. They believe this encourages local wages to rise. MNCs also claim to improve health and safety and other labour market conditions in the poor countries in which they operate **a c**.

But by threatening to close down factories and to move production to poor countries, it is argued that MNCs also reduce wages and living standards in First World countries. Whether this is true depends, of course, on the type of jobs that emerge in developed countries to replace those lost through deindustrialisation and globalisation. Are the new jobs created in the highly skilled service sector, or are they menial, low-paid, unskilled 'McJobs' **c**?

In recent decades, globalisation has considerably reduced the power of national governments, certainly in smaller countries, to control multinational firms operating within their boundaries. National governments have also lost much of the freedom to undertake the economic policies of their choice with respect to managing domestic economies. Governments enjoy less freedom to introduce tariffs and other import controls. At the same time, capital flows into and out of currencies severely constrain a government's ability to implement an independent monetary policy, even when the country's exchange rate is freely floating.

(e) **19/25 marks awarded.** In many ways this is a very good answer. **a** Indeed, at least some of the answer could have been included in the answer to part [11] to pick up the extra marks needed there for explanation. However, although containing lots of relevant knowledge and argument, the answer does not reach Level 5. This is because the student has not directly addressed key words in the question: 'must' and 'everybody'. **b** Obviously, not everybody gains from globalisation. The answer needs to indicate who the winners and losers are from the globalisation process. **c** There is some implicit debate of this issue, which enables the answer to reach Level 4. Winners and losers may vary, of course, depending on the state of the global economy and of individual nation states within the global economy. In the 2008 global recession, it was fashionable to argue that more and more losers were emerging. Also, the recession led to a fall in world trade and in capital flows between countries, along with a move towards greater protectionism. Some commentators argued that de-globalisation processes were replacing those of globalisation. Resumption of global economic growth should, however, reverse this process.

(e) **Scored 32/40: 80% = A* grade boundary**

Knowledge check answers

The growth of modern macroeconomics

1 Employment is the selling of labour in return for pay. Unemployment occurs when people without jobs are actively looking for paid work.

2 A free-market economy is a market economy in which the government does not intervene.

3 Fiscal policy uses the fiscal instruments of government spending and taxation. Monetary policy uses monetary instruments, particularly interest rates.

Economic growth, the economic cycle and living standards

4 A production possibility frontier shows the different combinations of output that can be produced by switching factors of production between different uses.

5 In the UK, the official definition of a recession is 6 months or more of falling real output. Other countries such as the USA and Japan have looser definitions. There is no official definition of a depression — it is just a long and deep recession, though other definitions have been suggested.

6 In the UK, economic cycles are deemed to begin and end when there is no output gap, positive or negative.

Aggregate demand and aggregate supply

7 Wealth is the *stock* of what people own; income is the *flow* of new wealth received over a particular time period.

8 To prevent booms which overheat the economy and lead to downturns in which unemployment grows. Stabilising the economic cycle may or may not lead to faster trend growth.

9 Increases in (i) consumption, (ii) investment, (iii) government spending and (iv) exports, together with (v) a fall in imports.

Unemployment and inflation

10 Since CPI inflation rises at a slower rate than RPI inflation, index-linked pensions etc. are likely to rise at a slower rate than before. This will save the government money.

11 Whereas equilibrium unemployment occurs at the natural rate of unemployment (NRU), disequilibrium unemployment, often known as real-wage unemployment, occurs when labour market imperfections prevent the NRU being achieved.

12 A consequence of unemployment, other than those mentioned on page 28, is that many of the long-term unemployed in effect become unemployable. They lose job-skills and/or fail to take on new skills, losing the personal characteristics that make firms want to hire them.

13 Shoe leather costs are the costs in terms of lost time and money that unemployed workers suffer when looking for new jobs. Part of the cause of shoe-leather costs is a lack of accurate and up-to-date information about what jobs are available.

The Phillips curve and the natural rate of unemployment

14 One conflict is the conflict between higher living standards *now* and higher living standards *in the future*. In the short term, the easiest way to increase living standards is to boost consumption. However, this means sacrificing saving and investment, which are the 'seed corn' of faster future growth and living standards.

15 Two causes are: (i) money wages rising faster than the rate of labour productivity growth, and (ii) the rising prices of imported energy, food, commodities and manufactured goods.

16 As stated in the answer to question 11, the natural rate of unemployment and the equilibrium level of unemployment are basically the same thing, though the former is measured as a *rate* and the latter as a *level* (see the answer to the next question).

17 The natural *level* of unemployment is the total number of frictionally unemployed workers when unemployment is at its equilibrium level, e.g. 1 million. By contrast, the natural *rate* of unemployment (NRU) expresses this figure as a percentage ratio of the total working population, e.g. 5%.

Monetary policy

18 When a person deposits cash in a bank, the bank now owns the cash but credits the customer's account with a bank deposit equal to this amount of cash. More bank deposits are created when other customers borrow from the bank. Through this process, bank deposits multiply to form a much larger proportion of the money supply than cash.

19 The credit crunch that started in 2007 was a sudden reduction in the general availability of credit or loans. It was caused by a dramatic and sudden tightening of the conditions required to obtain a bank loan. The credit crunch was made worse by bank collapses and by the fear of further collapses.

20 The main element of a monetarist monetary policy would be strictly controlling the rate of growth of the money supply in the event of an unacceptable rise (or feared rise) in inflation. Monetarist money policy could also follow the opposite route of increasing the money supply to prevent a shortage of money dragging the economy into recession.

Fiscal policy and supply-side policy

21 Demand-side policy is the use of fiscal and/or monetary policy to manage the level of aggregate demand. It is illustrated by shifts of the *AD* curve in the *AD/AS* macroeconomic model.

22 The investment multiplier measures the difference between an initial change in investment and the resulting change in national income. By contrast, the accelerator measures the opposite relationship: namely, that between an initial change in national income and the resulting change in investment.

23 In the recovery and boom phases (the upswing) of the economic cycle, tax revenues rise and demand-led spending on unemployment benefits falls, causing the budget deficit to shrink, with the government finances perhaps moving into surplus. In the downswing, the opposite process takes place, particularly if the downswing results in recession.

International trade, globalisation and the EU

24 The opportunity cost of any decision or action is the cost of the next best alternative sacrificed or forgone.

25 Economic welfare simply means human happiness, including happiness arising from consuming goods and services, and from intangibles such as the enjoyment of family and friends and looking at a beautiful view.

26 Increasing returns to scale occur when a doubling of the factors of production employed leads to a more than doubling of output. With decreasing returns to scale, the result is a less than doubling of output. Both are microeconomic concepts.

The balance of payments, exchange rates and the euro

27 An outward capital flow (investment flow) — for example, when a UK firm invests in an overseas subsidiary — generates an inward income flow when the subsidiary repatriates its profit to its UK parent firm. Likewise, an inward capital flow generates an outward income flow.

28 'Hot money' flows can destabilise exchange rates, and thence national economies. They can lead to grossly overvalued or undervalued exchange rates, which distort trading competitiveness in the economies affected.

29 In the long term, a current account deficit can be reduced or eliminated by an improvement in supply-side conditions in the economy (e.g. the country's goods and services becoming more quality competitive). In the short term, government policies such as devaluation of the exchange rate and imposing import controls can reduce a current account deficit.

Page numbers in **bold** refer to **key term definitions**